Crypto and Bitcoin

A Millionaire Mindset for Opportunity

Michael A. Duniec

ISBN: 979-8990830615/60 (Hardcovers) | ISBN: 979-8990830622/84/91 (Paperbacks)

ISBN: 979-8990830608 (eBook) | ISBN: 979-8990830639 (Audiobook)

U.S. Copyright: TX 9-394-146

Library of Congress Control Number: 2024910689

Published by Actimor LLC. Publishing Group, Ohio

𝕏 actimorbooks |ⓞ actimorpublishing | btcmindset.com

This book is proudly distributed in the United States and around the world. It is available in print, e-book, & audio formats.

Dedication

This book is dedicated to those whose journey through the digital frontier mirrors the very essence of innovation and perseverance. From the early days of Bitcoin, when virtual coins could be had for mere pennies and the world of cryptocurrency was a wild, uncharted expanse, to the tumultuous times of market upheavals and technological breakthroughs, this story is a testament to the bold and the brave. We mined not just for currency but for knowledge, diving deep into the mechanics of blockchain and the principles of self-custody and security.

The experiences, from the adrenaline of the mining rush to the sobering lessons of market crashes and the closure of platforms like Mt. Gox and Silk Road, have painted a vivid picture of the crypto era's infancy. We have seen fortunes rise and fall with the market's volatility, yet your wealth lies not in the coins amassed but in the rich tapestry of lessons learned and wisdom gained.

This book is dedicated to you and to all who dare to dream and toil in the shadows of giants, for it is in the quiet hum of your GPUs & ASICs and the soft glow of your monitors that the future is forged. To the innovators, the visionaries, the relentless seekers of the next frontier—may this story inspire you to chase the horizon, even when the world whispers of impossibility. In the pursuit of the seemingly unattainable, we uncover the paths to new worlds. Here's to the dreamers, the doers, and the digital pioneers—may your trails blaze bright and your legacies endure.

Acknowledgment

In the dynamic and ever-evolving world of cryptocurrency and decentralized finance, the creation of this book has been a journey of discovery, innovation, and deep learning. I am profoundly grateful to a community that thrives on the principles of openness and collaboration.

To the countless developers and miners who have laid the groundwork for this technology, your tireless dedication has propelled the industry forward and provided invaluable insights for the pages of this book.

A special thanks to the thought leaders and visionaries in the DeFi space; your bold ideas and unwavering commitment to reimagining financial systems have been a constant source of inspiration. To the seasoned and newcomer investors who have placed their trust in the potential of digital assets, your stories and experiences have been the cornerstone of this comprehensive guide.

I must also acknowledge the invaluable support of my peers and mentors in the crypto community, whose wisdom and guidance have been instrumental in navigating the complex landscape of blockchain technology. The contributions of academic researchers who have explored the theoretical underpinnings of cryptocurrency have enriched the content with a depth of knowledge that is both profound and practical. To my wife, daughters, and friends, for your patience and understanding as I ventured into the depths of writing and research; your support has been my anchor. And to the readers, who are the ultimate driving force behind this endeavor, may this book serve as a beacon, illuminating the path to financial empowerment and a new understanding of a Bitcoin Mindset.

About the Author

Mike, an early innovator in the cryptocurrency realm, embarked on his Bitcoin journey in 2011, during the nascent stages of digital currency when decentralized money was still a novel idea. With the price of Bitcoin at a mere seventy cents, Mike's foresight and determination led him to mine the cryptocurrency, leveraging the computational power of GPUs in an era where mining pools were the crux of Bitcoin acquisition. His story is not just about the triumphs but also the tribulations, including the infamous Mt. Gox hacks and the eventual shutdown of the Silk Road, which shaped his perspective on the volatility and the potential of this digital asset.

As the landscape evolved, so did Mike's strategies. He delved deeper into the blockchain technology that underpins Bitcoin, shifting from mining to a more analytical approach of acquiring coins through market purchases. A meticulous cost-benefit analysis of hardware and power investments versus retail market purchases drove this pivot. Mike's expertise extended beyond mere acquisition; he became a proponent of self-custody and robust security principles, advocating for a mix of hot and mainly cold hardware wallet storage to safeguard digital assets against the backdrop of a tumultuous market.

The common misconception that early Bitcoin miners like Mike must have amassed fortunes is challenged by the reality of the market's early instability. Despite mining Bitcoin when it was worth fractions of a dollar, Mike focused on the sustainable growth of his operation, ensuring that his endeavors could support his living expenses while fueling his passion for coding and optimization. The longing for a time machine is a sentiment shared by many early adopters, yet the lessons learned and experiences truly define Mike's journey.

Mike's tale is a testament to the spirit of innovation. His makeshift mining setup, consisting of GPUs jury-rigged in a cardboard box, might have seemed eccentric to his peers. Still, it was a beacon of the innovative drive that characterizes true pioneers. The skepticism he faced reinforced his belief that he was at the forefront of something groundbreaking. Mike's narrative is a compelling chronicle of the early days of cryptocurrency, offering readers a personal account of the trials and triumphs that come with being an innovator in a field once dismissed by many.

This book is more than a memoir; it is a historical account of cryptocurrency's infancy, an exploration of monetary principles, and a guide to government policies shaping the crypto landscape. It invites readers to delve into the crypto world, encouraging them to research and understand the intricacies of this revolutionary technology. Mike's story is not just about Bitcoin; it's about the relentless pursuit of innovation and the indomitable spirit of those who dare to envision a different financial future. It's a narrative that inspires, educates, and serves as a beacon for aspiring innovators in the crypto space and beyond.

With over a decade of immersion in the dynamic world of cryptocurrencies, Mike brings a wealth of firsthand experience. This book is not just a guide; it's a journey through the evolving landscape of DeFi, Web 3.0, and blockchain innovation, where rapid transactions with minimal fees are just the beginning.

Mike's passion for uncovering the myriad of untapped opportunities in the crypto space is palpable and serves as a beacon for aspiring enthusiasts. By adopting a Bitcoin mindset, readers will gain insights into recognizing potential, understanding cutting-edge technology, and exploring the burgeoning projects that emerge daily. This book is an invitation to explore, learn, and succeed in the crypto universe, and the author eagerly anticipates celebrating the reader's achievements and newfound knowledge.

Preface

In this comprehensive exploration of the digital currency revolution, we embark on a journey through the intricate world of cryptocurrencies. From the genesis of Bitcoin to the myriad of crypto-assets that have followed, this book delves into the technological innovation that has challenged traditional financial systems and sparked a global conversation about the future of money. Each chapter is a deep dive into the key moments and critical developments that have shaped the cryptocurrency landscape.

We begin with the birth of cryptocurrency, a disruptive concept that emerged from the shadows of the 2008 financial crisis, promising a new era of decentralized finance. As we move through the early years of Bitcoin, we witness the struggles and triumphs of a novel asset fighting for legitimacy. The development of cryptocurrency is a tale of innovation, as diverse as the people who contribute to its evolution. The impact on traditional banking is undeniable, as cryptocurrencies offer an alternative to established financial institutions, forcing them to adapt or risk obsolescence.

The role of central banks and government in this new financial frontier is complex, balancing the potential benefits with the need for regulation and stability. The volatility of cryptocurrency is both a lure for investors and a warning for the cautious, making it a fascinating study of market dynamics. The rise of crypto-assets and investment opportunities signals a shift in how we perceive value and investment in the digital age. Blockchain mining, while a cornerstone of cryptocurrency's functionality, raises pressing concerns about environmental sustainability.

As we look to the future of cryptocurrency, we are faced with questions about its integration into daily life and the long-term implications for global economies. In conclusion, this book is not just a historical account but a dialogue about the intersection of technology, economics, society, and innovation mindsets—a conversation that is only just beginning through the eyes of Roger.

Additionally, this publication provides a Glossary that serves as a valuable tool for clarifying technical jargon, terms unique to cryptocurrency, tech, and specialized financial terminology.

Contents

Dedication... i

Acknowledgment.. ii

About the Author.. iv

Preface...vii

Introduction... 1

Chapter 1: The Birth of Cryptocurrency............................. 10

Chapter 2: The Early Years of Bitcoin................................. 31

Chapter 3: The Development of Cryptocurrency.................. 50

Chapter 4: The Impact of Cryptocurrency on Traditional Banking 66

Chapter 5: The Role of Central Banks and Government...................... 83

Chapter 6: The Volatility of Cryptocurrency 102

Chapter 7: The Rise of Crypto-Assets and Investment Opportunities127

Chapter 8: Blockchain Mining and its Impact on the Environment ... 150

Chapter 9: The Future of Cryptocurrency........................... 169

Chapter 10: Conclusion... 186

Glossary 200

Introduction

Roger sat in his apartment sipping on the piping hot coffee he had made.

He asked himself what a morning would be without a coffee, then reclined on the couch to enjoy the pleasant weather. Since it was Sunday, he didn't have much work to do and had decided not to turn on his laptop until the next day. As he sipped the coffee, he remembered that the price of the coffee had almost doubled since he last bought it due to inflation.

If the central bank continued minting U.S. Dollars and expanding the money supply, depreciating it in the process, inflation would never stop. His gaze settled on the bookcase that had been a part of his life for more than ten years, and he thought *that if only cryptocurrencies had been incorporated into the system, the problem of inflation might have been mitigated since the bitcoin system, unlike traditional banking and payment systems, is based on decentralized trust.*[1] While glancing at the bookshelf, he set his eyes on a book, "Mastering Bitcoin," that he had read back in 2017. Having another sip of the coffee, he walked towards the bookshelf and grabbed the book, glancing at its contents.

Some key terms, such as decentralized digital currency, peer-to-peer network, proof of work, and blockchain, flashed past his eyes. With each term, he had a flashback of how he got an introduction to it and how it affected his financial practices in the modern world. The first term that caught his attention was decentralized digital currency—the term that changed his life. He still remembered that amidst the financial crisis of 2008, the rave about cryptocurrencies took the world by storm.

After the banking systems and financial institutions failed to recover large mortgages lent to homeowners, the emergence of cryptocurrency was deemed as an alternative to address the flaws in the existing monetary systems.

However, Roger didn't know about it until 2012, when he heard about the concept of decentralized digital currency from his friend.

"It's the other name for the cryptocurrencies, the digital currency, that isn't regularized or centralized by any authority such as a central bank," he remembered his friend telling him, who had been entirely invested in learning about cryptocurrency since Satoshi's document emerged in 2009, which was known as the Bitcoin Whitepaper. He was the one who introduced him to Bitcoin, too. *"Unlike traditional currencies, bitcoin is entirely virtual. There are no physical coins or even digital coins per se. The coins are implied in transactions that transfer value from the sender to recipient,"*[2] he had read somewhere while searching about Bitcoin.

As he glanced through the book, he realized how much had changed in the world of cryptocurrency in the last ten years. From being a novel and suspicious idea to becoming an integral part of the practical world, how far had the world come, and how far had he come as a cryptocurrency miner and developer? He sighed and put the book back on the shelf. While returning to his couch, his eyes fall on the calendar displaying May 22.

Ah! It's Bitcoin Pizza Day, the day Laszlo Hanyecz bought two large pizzas for 10,000 Bitcoins, he exclaimed, and instead of going towards his couch, he came back towards the shelf.

Bitcoin—how strangely interesting this currency is, which is created through mining and verified on the blockchain. If Laszlo Hanyecz had those Bitcoins today, they would have been worth roughly $200 million. Anyone reading this book today could never resonate with how I understood the nitty-gritty of cryptocurrency and Bitcoin a decade ago, he thought while looking at the book. Understanding Bitcoin and cryptocurrency seemed more difficult in 2014 since there wasn't enough research on the topic, and people also lacked first-hand experience using it.

The fact that *"users can transfer bitcoin over the network to do just about anything that can be done with conventional currencies, including buying and selling goods, sending money to people or organizations, or extending credit"*[3] was a hard pill to swallow for many. Moreover, the concepts of bitcoin transactions and bitcoin mining were also complicated for the people. Roger understood mining as *"a giant competitive game of sudoku that resets every time someone finds a solution and whose difficulty automatically adjusts so that it takes approximately 10 minutes to find a solution."*[4] It then made it easier for him to understand how mining secures Bitcoin transactions by verifying valid transactions and rejecting malformed or invalid transactions. Moreover, it creates new bitcoins in each block, similar to how the central bank prints currency. However, he knew that with the abundance of information and many advancements, understanding these concepts and the practical knowledge of how to implement them in your life seems even more challenging.

He realized that there must be a comprehensive yet practical and informative yet relatable blueprint to help people navigate the complexities of cryptocurrencies and find a way to leverage their knowledge to improve their financial positions. He then looked at his laptop and realized he had enough knowledge and hands-on experience to compile something valuable for the world.

He knew that it was not going to happen overnight. Although it had been a little over ten years of crypto, there were still developers, innovators, enthusiasts, and people who had a lot of hardship through the banking crisis who would want to explore this world. After spending adequate time in this space, he knew that educating more people was still a need.

"The world needs to understand the history and fundamentals behind Bitcoin, and I would keep spreading the word," he said to himself and opened a blank document to draft his thoughts. He understood that some of the technical complexities and novel concepts could be daunting at first. Still, it would be nearly impossible to realize the actual potential of that space without diving deep into the theory and history behind blockchain projects like Bitcoin and Ethereum. It is crucial to understand the cryptocurrency world to push past the fear of the unknown and recognize crypto's enormous potential to transform finance positively.

An average person needs to understand the basic concepts to wrap their hands around the crypto space. *I have been in the crypto space for so long that it now feels like a sin if I don't educate people about its opportunities and prospects. But where should I start?* he thought, and his mind drifted back to 2009 when Satoshi Nakamoto's whitepaper created a buzz in the world about the potential of decentralized digital currencies. Not only did the author's anonymity gain attention, but the details of the whitepaper were also compelling enough to gain massive responses from people. Right after the burst of the housing market bubble created by the banks and the financial institutions in the U.S., the world has been eagerly looking for a solution to take them out of the financial adversities.

As Roger began to type out his thoughts, he recounted the highs and lows, the technological breakthroughs, and the societal shifts that had shaped the crypto world.

During the financial crisis, cryptocurrency emerged as a savior in the Wild West and caught people's attention as the solution to the drawbacks of fiat money. Unlike commodity money, where the currency's intrinsic value lies in the material with which it is manufactured, such as gold or silver coins, fiat money's inherent value lies in public faith and decree of its mandatory use by the issuer, i.e., the government. Since fiat money isn't backed by any valuable commodity such as gold or silver, the risk of its devaluation during inflation is always there. The first decade of the evolution of cryptocurrency was full of exciting discoveries and innovations that transformed the world and financial practices. However, entering that world seemed like an uphill task for novice individuals, such as non-technical individuals with no programming or developing knowledge or experience.

The whitepaper released by the pseudonymous developers became the foundation for developing a model for a blockchain introducing blockchain technology to the world. Along with the publication of the Bitcoin whitepaper, bitcoin, the first cryptocurrency, was introduced to the public as "*a collection of concepts and technologies that form the basis of a digital money ecosystem where units of currency called bitcoin are used to store and transmit value among participants in the Bitcoin network.*"[5]

Despite people initially being skeptical about cryptocurrency, the evolution and growth of the cryptocurrency ecosystem and the introduction of new cryptocurrencies, such as Litecoin and Ethereum, created viable opportunities for those who realized its true potential. Success stories of people like Charlie Shrem spoke volumes about how the innovation within the space had been immersed. Going into that innovation, the rise of smart contracts created a breakthrough, paving the way for more advanced protocols like DeFi contracts, Web 3.0, and Polygon (MATIC) Chains, the cheaper (gas fees) platform for cryptocurrency transactions.

The evolution of money, starting from paper money backed by gold to digital currency, has taken many forms, solved various problems, and brought multiple opportunities. However, in modern times, most money is fiat, like the U.S. dollar, and it's created and regulated by the central bank and government. The system relies heavily on trust and the institutions to manage monetary policy. The reliance of the whole economy on the whims of bureaucrats and not real tangible assets is one of the leading causes of significant problems in the economic system that cryptocurrency can solve.

However, it is not always the golden solution when it comes to cryptocurrencies. Despite the promising potential, cryptocurrency has had various pitfalls, too. For instance, the high volatility, lack of regulations, and cyber-attacks are the significant drawbacks casting dark shadows on the potential of cryptocurrency. Yet, against all odds and predictions of the failure of Bitcoin and cryptocurrencies, Bitcoin survived over the decade and thrived. Therefore, understanding the space, along with all its intricacies and ebb and flow, allows potential entrants to become aware of the challenges they might have to navigate.

Despite notable advancements in the fields, the rules of the road regarding crypto are still being written. The currency that initially started as an entirely unregulated currency went through several stages of growth and development to regulate the industry over the decade. The regulatory departments and authorities, including SEC, CFTC, IRS, and others, are still working to set regulations regarding crypto mining, taxation, regulation, and other relevant policies regarding cryptocurrency. Besides the U.S., sophisticated cryptocurrency regulations have attracted significant startups in other first-world countries like Singapore, Caymans, and Switzerland. As technology keeps shaping and the cryptocurrency revolution continues, the potential for wealth-building also strengthens. Although the future remains unwritten, if anyone understands the landscape of crypto's origins today, they can fully participate in the new world of finance, ensuring their journey ahead will be rewarding.

By the time Roger finished writing his draft and looked at the clock, around three hours had passed.

He had so much on his mind that he wanted to share with the world, teaching them how to leverage his knowledge and pave their way towards financial independence and wealth building that he couldn't wait to share with others.

His half-finished cup of coffee resting on the table caught his attention. Immersed in jotting down his thoughts, he had forgotten about the coffee that had turned cold. However, he was content with reading what he had written. It seemed like the perfect opening of the book, with different chapters breaking down complex concepts into understandable ideas.

Beginning with the birth of cryptocurrency and the early years of Bitcoin, he planned on shedding light on the development of cryptocurrency and its various types. He was eager to share his experience with Bitcoin mining to clear the air around it. Building on that, he decided to dissect the impact of cryptocurrency on traditional banking and the role of central banks and the government. Finally, he would uncover the opportunities and risks in cryptocurrency, giving readers a blueprint for navigating the crypto world to make the most of it. Little did he know that his journey would become a narrative, a story told not in graphs and charts but through the lens of a person's first-hand experience, navigating the complexities of the crypto universe.

Chapter 1: The Birth of Cryptocurrency

"49,980.20 USD," the numbers flashing on the screen made Roger smile as he checked the current worth of a Bitcoin. It reminded him of the early days of cryptocurrencies like Bitcoin when nobody was prepared to buy one, and it had no set value.

It was around October 31, 2008, a year after the outset of the great recession, while the severe economic downturn and the ugly time in money and finance continued. People were striving to make ends meet and looking for a solution to end the financial turmoil that no one had seen coming. However, the economic system's sudden crash wasn't so "sudden." In reality, it had been a build-up of several years destined to end the same way it ended. People were naming various reasons as the culprits for bursting the U.S. housing bubble, but Roger believed that the main culprits were the creators of that bubble—the banks and the banking system.

The allure of the American Dream cost a price higher than what people had expected. As the government failed to regulate the financial industry, banks went on a spree to grant credit on lenient terms and low interest rates, causing an abnormal increase in demand. Banks lent mortgages without considering the borrowers' bad credit risk and creditworthiness.

Anticipating that the interest rates would always remain low and the real estate prices would keep increasing, even those who wouldn't have otherwise qualified for the loan got the credit at low interest rates. The dramatic surge in the volume of total mortgages and the introduction of unsecured financial innovations, such as adjustable mortgages and subprime loans, caused the volume of credit issued to borrowers to increase dramatically. As the government increased the interest rates to curb the surging inflation, the interest rates on the existing adjustable mortgages and exotic loans increased significantly. It grew to a level that exceeded the borrowers' expectations and ability to repay, causing many borrowers to default. Due to their inability to pay off their mortgages, people began selling their properties, causing an abnormal surge in supply with negligible demand.

The collapse in the U.S. housing market led to a collapse in the value of mortgage-backed securities floating in the market. Large investment banks and financial institutions began collapsing one after the other, spreading the economic downturn to other economies worldwide like an epidemic. As a result of the economic recession, people lost trust in the banking and monetary system.

That's when cryptic news of the publication of the Bitcoin whitepaper took the whole country by storm.

"Satoshi Nakamoto's Bitcoin: A new dawn for money?" Roger felt compelled to click on that news out of curiosity to learn the details. As he explored the news details, he found a whitepaper outlining the announcement of a decentralized currency entirely different from the prevailing centralized system.

A person named Satoshi Nakamoto sent a paper called "Bitcoin: A Peer-to-Peer Electronic Cash System" to a cryptography mailing list, announcing the public advent of Bitcoin to the world. He presented a *"purely peer-to-peer version of electronic cash that would allow online payments to be sent directly from one party to another without going through a financial institution."*[6] After saving the document to study at a later time, he searched for the author. *"Who is Satoshi Nakamoto?"*

Roger stared at the screen, reading and rereading the whitepaper titled "Bitcoin: A Peer-to-Peer Electronic Cash System." He leaned back in his chair, fingers steepled in thought as he mulled over the potential implications.

"This could change everything," he murmured.

The document outlined a revolutionary digital currency system that allowed online payments to be sent directly between parties without the need for a financial institution. It was brilliant in its simplicity—using cryptography and a distributed timestamp server to generate computational proof of the chronological order of transactions.

But who was this Satoshi Nakamoto? The paper provided no information about its author, name, or email address—only a cryptographic public key.

Roger furrowed his brow, deep in speculation. Was Nakamoto an individual or a group? American, European, Asian? The Japanese-sounding pseudonym offered no real clues.

Checking the timestamp, Roger saw that the paper was published on October 31, 2008. He thought back to the financial crisis that had been worsening over the past month. Major banks were failing left and right while the stock market plummeted. People were losing trust in traditional financial institutions.

"Perfect timing," Roger muttered. "This could be the antidote—a decentralized system, free from intermediaries." A way to transfer funds securely without relying on banks or governments. Revolutionary.

That's the question that surrounded the minds of everyone who learned about the news. Everyone was curious to know about him but could not get a trace of his real identity. Roger ran a Google search for his name but couldn't get any beneficial results. That made Roger believe the name was a pseudonym purposely used to conceal the author's real identity. He had no idea, back then, that the realm of cryptocurrencies had given rise to one of the greatest mysteries of the twenty-first century, one that is still unanswered to this day.

The information revealed in the whitepaper couldn't go unnoticed. Therefore, people were curious to know about the individual who had cracked cryptographers' decade-old problem by creating a decentralized digital currency liberated from the control of a central authority. As curiosity rose among people, different conspiracy theories began coming to light about the identity of the author of the Bitcoin whitepaper, Satoshi Nakamoto. One of the first presumptions was that the person in question was a group of individuals or businesses rather than an individual. Since the pronoun "we" was used throughout the whitepaper, it strengthened the claims of Satoshi being a group instead of an individual.

However, no one could trace the people involved in that group. The only mode of communication used by Satoshi was email. With the lack of background details and personal information, tracing the origins of Satoshi seemed nearly impossible, but the quest never halted. More theories were added with time, and some suspicions were even placed on different people. One of the first persons believed to be Satoshi Nakamoto was a Japanese-American man due to his libertarian leanings, Japanese heritage, and his last name. The earliest bits of information revealed about Satoshi Nakamoto was that he possibly lived in Japan. However, the email address he used was believed to be from a German-based service. Dorian Nakamoto, a physics graduate from California Polytechnic, vehemently denied the accusations of him being Satoshi.

Another strong claim about finding out Satoshi's true identity was made about an Australian scientist, Craig Wright when a magazine claimed to have strong evidence. The most convincing evidence was Wright's blogs, which referenced a cryptocurrency paper months before the publication of the Bitcoin whitepaper. Some leaked emails, correspondence, and transcripts of meetings with his lawyers also hinted at him being the mastermind behind the Bitcoin fiasco. It was later found out that the blog entries were backdated, which created a strong argument against the suspicion of him being the real Satoshi.

Later on, Nick Szabo, the founder of Bit Gold, also came under the radar of suspicions. He not only pioneered the idea of smart contracts in a 1996 paper, but his concept of Bit Gold was also pretty similar to Bitcoin. Some other similarities also hinted at Nick's possible real identity, but no substantial evidence could have corroborated the claims.

Another interesting theory Roger came across was about Satoshi Nakamoto, which is the acronym for four Asian companies: Samsung, Toshiba, Nakamichi, and Motorola. People believed that the four tech companies might have a hand in publishing the Bitcoin whitepaper but couldn't find enough evidence to support this belief. People even thought of him as a time traveler or an alien who disappeared after publishing the whitepaper. The identity of Satoshi remains a mystery to date. Even over a decade since the introduction of Bitcoin, people are clueless about who Satoshi is and the real motive behind his hidden identity.

After rummaging about the mysterious author of the Bitcoin whitepaper, Roger got his hands back on the contents of the paper. Sitting on his chair in front of the computer, he leaned forward, reading with renewed excitement. Paragraph by paragraph, the technical details began to make sense. This was more than just theory—the paper described a working system. Whoever Nakamoto was had already created software to implement the Bitcoin protocol. As he scanned through the paper, he realized that it outlined a solution to the double-spending problem by introducing the world's first decentralized digital currency. The paper started by highlighting the limitations of electronic payment systems and the cons of reliance on third-party intermediaries.

"While the system works well enough for most transactions, it still suffers from the inherent weaknesses of the trust-based model. Completely non-reversible transactions are not really possible since financial institutions cannot avoid mediating disputes."[7]

As a solution to the above-stated problem, Satoshi highlighted the need for a purely peer-to-peer electronic cash system that would eliminate the need for trusted third parties.

"What is needed is an electronic payment system based on cryptographic proof instead of trust, allowing any two willing parties to transact directly without needing a trusted third party."

He then introduced the idea of a digital coin, which he defined as *'a chain of digital signatures.'* As Roger kept reading, his curiosity increased. He proceeded to the next section of the paper, which discussed the transactions.

Unlike the traditional system, which relied on one entity to check and approve transactions, Satoshi put out a mechanism that would require transactions to be made public for verification. Following his whitepaper, before each transaction block (a public transaction ledger) was added to the blockchain, all parties involved had to agree on and record the transaction's sequence.

"But how can it be done?" exclaimed Roger as he proceeded to the next section.

"The solution we propose begins with a timestamp server,"[8] the first sentence caught his attention. Bitcoin solved the double-spending problem by providing evidence of the presence of each block on the blockchain referencing a timestamp. According to his proposal, all the information stored in the Bitcoin block was crunched into a shorter string of characters known as a hash. Every block's hash would also contain the previous block's hash, and a Bitcoin miner adding a new block to the blockchain would timestamp the hash. With each hash reinforcing and verifying the previous hash, the risk of unverified transactions would be eliminated.

The mechanism to prevent double-spending and verify each transaction was called "proof-of-work." The Bitcoin network would use *"a distributed computation system (called a proof-of-work algorithm) to conduct a global election every 10 minutes, allowing the decentralized network to reach a consensus about the state of transactions. This solves the issue of double-spend where a single unit of currency can be sold twice"*[9]

The whitepaper defined it as a one-CPU, one-vote system where honest nodes would lead to an open blockchain. The six steps to run the Bitcoin network mentioned in the paper included:

- *New transactions are broadcast to all nodes.*

- *Each node collects new transactions into a block.*

- *Each node works on finding a difficult proof-of-work for its block.*

- *When a node finds a proof-of-work, it broadcasts the blocks to all nodes.*

- *Nodes accept the block only if all transactions in it are valid and have not already been spent.*

- *Nodes express their acceptance of the block by creating the next block in the chain, using the accepted block's hash as the previous one.[10]*

Roger understood it as every participant in the Bitcoin network seeing and verifying the transactions to ensure transparency and security. *"Mining provides security for bitcoin transactions by rejecting invalid or malformed transactions. It creates new bitcoin in each block just like a central bank printing new money."[11]*

The following section revealed the incentive-based mining framework. In order to encourage nodes to remain honest, the system would add an incentive for the nodes to support the network.

"What does that mean?" he pondered until he understood it.

"Minning achieves a fine balance between cost and reward. Mining uses electricity to solve a mathematical problem. A successful miner will collect a reward in the form of a new bitcoin and a transaction fee. However, the reward will only be collected

if the miner has correctly validated all the transactions, to the satisfaction of the rules of the consensus."[12]

The older Bitcoin transactions were proposed to be hashed into a summary of multiple transactions (Merkle Trees) to reclaim the disk space and simplify the payment verification process for the nodes. Instead of making separate transactions for every transfer, each transaction would have either a single input from a larger previous transaction or multiple smaller inputs and two outputs. One output is for the payment, and the other is for returning the change.

Lastly, he came across the part where he was most concerned about—privacy. Unlike traditional banking systems, Bitcoin transactions are based on the complete anonymity of the account owner. Each account owner would receive a distinct address, or what is known as the public key, which is a string of 26–35 characters. Every node could see the transactions without knowing the payee's identity. The unique address assigned to every account owner would not be linked to any private information of the account owner.

"One of the advantages of Bitcoin over other payment systems is that, when used correctly, it affords users much more privacy. Acquiring, holding, and spending bitcoin does not require you to divulge sensitive and personally identifiable information to third parties."[13]

On the other hand, the account owner will have a private key, an alphanumeric code similar to a password, to access their

Bitcoin wallets, authorize transactions, and prove ownership of a blockchain asset. Roger's mind raced as he contemplated the ramifications.

"This could give people financial sovereignty and privacy. Cut out the middlemen fees charged by payment processors. Provide accessibility to anyone with an internet connection. Bank the unbanked. Empower the individual," Roger's eyes lit up as he comprehended the idea of the digital ledger.

"That also means that the person's phone can get destroyed, but as long as they have their secret key, they can return to the network and recreate their stored value. So, as long as you know your seed key, you could transfer wealth and store that wealth on the blockchain, which is your digital ledger, and nobody can take that from you," the more time he spent on it, the more he grasped the concept of the decentralized digital currency.

The paper revealed that *"Nakamoto combined several prior inventions such as b-money and HashCash to create a completely decentralized electronic cash system that does not rely on a central authority for currency issuance and settlement and validations of transactions."*[14] That meant that the decentralized digital currency would have the potential to fundamentally disrupt and reshape global finance.

"If the proposed system takes over the existing monetary system, the central banks and the governments would no longer have unilateral control over the money supply," Roger's curiosity grew a little more into the cryptocurrency as he saw it as a solution to resolve the flaws in the traditional financial system and a lot of hidden potential too. He could hardly wait to share this discovery with colleagues. If implemented correctly, Bitcoin could have a seismic impact. It could fundamentally change the nature of money and finance.

"This is just the beginning," Roger whispered to himself. He could feel it in his bones that Satoshi Nakamoto's paper represented a watershed moment—the dawn of a new era in decentralized digital currency. The future starts now. Moments later, Roger leaned back in his chair, rubbing his eyes as he tried to process everything he had just read. Satoshi Nakamoto's whitepaper was dense and technical, but the implications were profound.

This Bitcoin protocol could revolutionize finance by creating a peer-to-peer electronic cash system that doesn't rely on any central authority like a bank or government. It leveraged cryptographic proof and a distributed timestamp server to verify transactions. Bitcoin could be sent directly between users, like digital cash, without going through any financial institution. Roger glanced out the window at the city streets below. The global economy was still reeling from the 2008 financial crisis. Predatory lending practices by big banks triggered a massive real estate bubble that eventually burst, sending shockwaves throughout the system. The government had to step in with bailouts when overleveraged banks started failing. The Federal Reserve fired up the money printing presses in quantitative easing programs designed to inject liquidity into the struggling system.

"Quantitative Easing (QE) is a monetary policy tool that involves central banks buying financial assets from the market, typically government bonds or other securities, to inject money into the economy and lower long-term interest rates."[15] This policy is typically employed when the standard monetary policy measures, lowering interest rates, prove ineffective. Since most banks usually follow the fractional reserve banking system, the aim was to bail out, issue more loans to individuals and businesses, and prompt economic growth. In fractional reserve banking, only a fraction of customer deposits are held in reserve, while the rest is available for lending or investment. This system allows banks to create money through the process of lending, contributing to the overall money supply in the economy.

However, all the Fed's actions did was prop up the same big banks that caused the crisis in the first place. The little guys, average investors, and businesses on Main Street were left holding the bag. Banks didn't lend as much money as the Fed had hoped and were busy hoarding the cash.

Some banks utilized the accumulated funds to minimize the remaining subprime mortgage debt on their books, while others increased their capital ratios. Some banks even complained of not having enough credit-worthy borrowers due to raised lending standards. On the other hand, the QE program's liquidity added to the economic system didn't prove to be enough to increase the loans in circulation or the money supply.

Bitcoin offered an alternative—a decentralized monetary system that didn't rely on fallible human institutions. Its fixed supply and mining rewards meant no arbitrary printing of money or manipulation by central bankers, while users could control their funds without oversight by banks or governments.

"This can change everything," Roger exclaimed. Bitcoin could be the lifeboat to escape a sinking legacy financial system. It opened up a whole new realm of possibilities.

Roger knew he had to get involved and help share Bitcoin with the world. This was too important to keep quiet. He leaned forward again, eager to keep reading Satoshi's whitepaper and start figuring out how to support this technological revolution.

Roger spent the next few days deciphering the whitepaper. He leaned back in his chair, letting the weight of Satoshi's words sink in. This was no ordinary whitepaper—it outlined a framework for a decentralized digital currency and peer-to-peer payment system, unlike anything that existed before.

His thoughts drifted back to the origins of money, the *"universally accepted medium of exchange that serves as a unit of account, a store of value, and a standard of deferred payment,"*[16] and how much it has evolved over human history. Money has taken various forms throughout history, being a fundamental tool in economic systems and facilitating the exchange of goods and services by acting as an intermediary in transactions. From rudimentary barter systems prevailing around 6,000 years ago to precious metals and, eventually, paper money backed by gold, the currency has taken many forms.[17] However, in modern times, most money is fiat currency, like the U.S. dollar, created and regulated by central banks and governments.

This system relies heavily on trust in institutions to manage monetary policy responsibly. Yet, time and again, Roger had seen how central banks print money at will, devaluing savings and causing inflation (a hidden tax). The whole economy rests on the whims of bureaucrats, not any real tangible asset. Bitcoin is different. By design, only 21 million bitcoins will ever exist. New coins are "mined" by users, providing computing power to secure the network and process transactions through proof-of-work. The rules of the system are hardcoded - no human middlemen can alter the money supply.

The decentralized blockchain ledger allows for peer-to-peer transactions without centralized intermediaries, giving users control of their own money. Additionally, bitcoins have verifiable scarcity and can't be debased, making them an ideal store of value.

Roger smiled, feeling a rush of excitement. This wasn't just a new digital currency—it had the potential to change global finance and empower the individual fundamentally. The legacy banking system's days were numbered, and the future that Satoshi outlined was too revolutionary to ignore. Roger knew he had to be a part of that. In retrospect to the initial days of the launch of the publication of the Bitcoin whitepaper after a decade, Roger knew that his understanding of the paper's significance wasn't wrong. The significance of the Bitcoin whitepaper is multifaceted and extends far beyond simply being a technical document outlining a new digital currency. The whitepaper wasn't just explaining a new currency; it proposed an entirely new paradigm for online payments and value transfer. It introduced the idea of a decentralized, trustless digital currency, challenging the established financial system.

Pondering the implications of Bitcoin, Roger leaned back in his chair. *He thought about a decentralized digital currency outside the control of governments and banks.* It presented an intriguing way for people to exchange value peer-to-peer without relying on fallible intermediaries. Yet Roger knew there were challenges ahead. For Bitcoin to gain wide adoption, it needed to be easy for people to acquire and use it. That meant finding ways to convert fiat currencies like dollars into crypto—and vice versa.

Traditional currencies, also known as fiat currencies, are issued with the authorization of governments and central banks. Fiat money has no intrinsic value, as it is derived from the central authority that declares it legal tender. The central banks have the authority to print currency notes and circulate money in the market to keep the wheels of the economy running. The forces of supply and demand significantly impact the value of the fiat currency. The more money in circulation, the lesser its value, leading to inflation.

On the other hand, there is the idea of a decentralized currency that requires no regulation by any governmental authority. Decentralized currencies, like Bitcoin, drive their value from the community's trust. Unlike traditional currencies, bitcoin is protected from inflation risk through Bitcoin halving.[18] After the mining of every 210,000 blocks, the Bitcoin block reward is cut in half. As a result, the number of coins entering the network is reduced, reducing the risk of devaluation of the coin.

Cryptocurrencies serve as a means of exchange outside the traditional banking system by operating on decentralized networks, utilizing blockchain technology, and offering a borderless and inclusive financial alternative. By providing a decentralized and accessible means of exchange, they offer an alternative monetary system that operates outside the traditional banking framework. Cryptocurrencies operate on decentralized networks on the blockchain with no central authority controlling or governing the currency, such as a government or banking institution. They are accessible to anyone with an internet connection, regardless of their geographical location. This inclusivity allows individuals who may be unbanked or underbanked to participate in financial transactions without relying on traditional banking infrastructure.

Moreover, cryptocurrencies provide an alternative for individuals who do not have access to traditional banking services, reducing the need for intermediaries and potentially lowering transaction costs. Unlike traditional banking systems that may have operating hours and settlement periods, cryptocurrencies operate 24/7. Users can initiate transactions at any time, providing flexibility and convenience. However, the first step is to convert fiat currency into crypto to reap the benefits of cryptocurrencies. The process of converting fiat currency into crypto is called "on-ramping."[19] It is the entry point for individuals entering the cryptocurrency ecosystem from the fiat world, allowing them to acquire digital assets by purchasing them with traditional money. Exchanges and brokers like Coinbase simplify bank transfers, and you can buy Bitcoin. However, they required rigorous identity verification to comply with anti-money laundering regulations. Roger understood the need to prevent illicit activity but hated how the legacy banking system could freeze funds and deny service on a whim. Crypto promised financial freedom—yet on-ramps still relied on the very institutions Bitcoin sought to bypass.

The process of converting crypto back into fiat or entering the fiat world from the crypto ecosystem is called "off-ramping." This presented challenges, too. One of those challenges was related to compliance with KYC rules. KYC, or Know Your Customer, is a regulatory process that financial institutions implement to verify the identity of their customers. The primary goals of KYC procedures are to prevent fraud, money laundering, and other illicit activities. Bitcoin transactions were pseudonymous, making it hard for exchanges to comply with know-your-customer (KYC) rules. However, without off-ramps, crypto couldn't fulfill its mission of becoming "digital cash."

Roger knew this space was still the Wild West. But he was convinced that Bitcoin could revolutionize finance. There were regulatory issues to navigate, for sure, but he believed that it was early days. With time and scaling, Bitcoin could reshape how money flows across the world, unshackling individuals from centralized control. Roger was determined to make that vision a reality.

Besides authoring the Bitcoin whitepaper, Satoshi Nakamoto is credited for creating the first cryptocurrency blockchain in 2009, the Genesis block. It served as the first implication of the proof-of-work blockchain system proposed in the Bitcoin whitepaper and became a template for the other blocks later built on that blockchain. By 2009, the economic conditions began improving, marking the end of the Great Recession. That's when Satoshi Nakamoto launched the blockchain boom with the Genesis Block.

On January 3, 2009, Satoshi Nakamoto launched the Bitcoin network by mining the first block, known as the "Genesis Block," containing a message referencing the ongoing financial crisis.[20]

Roger recalled the launch and early days of the Bitcoin network as a fascinating period marked by excitement, technical challenges, and slow initial adoption.

He was glued to his computer screen as the first Bitcoin blocks were mined in January 2009. Luckily, he was one of the few people in the world aware of Satoshi Nakamoto's groundbreaking whitepaper, which proposed a revolutionary "peer-to-peer electronic cash system." Initially, only a handful of cryptographers and programmers were mining bitcoins on their personal computers. They were scattered around the world— unaware of each other's identities but united by a shared vision set forth by the mysterious Satoshi. Although people were on the verge of losing trust in the government-backed currency, adopting a currency with no backing from a central authority still sounded like the right choice. The initial transactions primarily involved sending small amounts of Bitcoin amongst developers and interested individuals.

The early Bitcoin network was fragile, with low hash rates that left it vulnerable to attack. But Roger had faith in Nakamoto's protocol, designed to incentivize miners to increase security over time. Transactions were agonizingly slow in these early days, taking hours to process. But it was functional enough to prove Bitcoin worked.

In October 2009, the New Liberty Standard set the first real-world BTC price at $1 = 1,309.03 BTC.[21] Roger remembered reading about a software developer, Martti Malmi, who sold 5,050 BTC for a $5.02 PayPal transfer, marking the first time that Bitcoin was exchanged for fiat currency. This demonstrated Bitcoin's utility as a payment system. However, later on, that transaction proved to be worth almost $200+ million.

Yet many challenges lay ahead. Bitcoin faced skepticism and hostility from mainstream finance. The concept of digital money with no centralized authority was unprecedented, and the system was still in its initial phase, with no friendly interfaces. However, Roger was undeterred, convinced that Bitcoin's transparency, immutability, and monetary autonomy made it the future. He dedicated himself to nurturing this fledgling technology, investing in startups, and promoting mainstream adoption. Roger knew Bitcoin would evolve, its capabilities expanding in ways even Nakamoto could not predict. But it had taken a monumental leap forward. The world had a decentralized option for government-issued currency. And there was no turning back from that.

Chapter 2: The Early Years of Bitcoin

Now that Roger had gathered enough information about the basics of Bitcoin and cryptocurrency, he decided to get into it. He knew that *"units of bitcoin are created through a process called "mining," which involves repeatedly performing a computational task that references a list of recent bitcoin transactions."*[22] Moreover, his understanding expanded to the fact that *"instead of a central trusted authority, in Bitcoin, each user can use software running on their own computer to verify the correct operation of every aspect of the Bitcoin system."*[23] Investigating the Bitcoin system, he learned that it is composed of three elements: users with wallets who possess keys to the bitcoins, transactions performed and disseminated across the network, and the miners who produce the blockchain of all transactions.

With the hope of exploiting the capabilities of the newly launched cryptocurrency, Roger began exploring the mainstream adoption options for Bitcoin. As he deep-dived into the market, he realized there weren't enough ways to obtain the novel money. The few available means contained significant risks for the users. Expanding his search, he discovered two ways to get Bitcoin—the first was to mine it himself, while the second involved engaging in a peer-to-peer (P2P) trade via cryptocurrency forums such as Bitcointalk[24]—a public forum founded by Satoshi Nakamoto that offers Bitcoin enthusiasts, developers, programmers, and investors the opportunity to engage in valuable conversations.

"Another development by the mysterious Satoshi," Roger murmured as he searched through the web to access the website. The platform was launched in the same year as the launch of Bitcoin and hosted discussions about cryptocurrency, blockchain, and Bitcoin. "What a treasure trove I've got my hands on," Roger couldn't contain his elation, as if he hit a jackpot. For a year, it became his go-to platform to learn about Bitcoin and keep an eye on all the upcoming updates and developments. Other developers, programmers, and people interested in Bitcoin actively engaged in insightful discussions. Roger's interest in cryptocurrency and Bitcoin grew even more as the year passed.

However, the early years of adoption and usage of Bitcoin were marked with several challenges. Public awareness was initially limited, and initial use cases were primarily speculative or technical experiments. The early years saw slow growth in user base and transaction volume. Additionally, mining was focused in the hands of a few individuals, raising concerns about centralization and potential manipulation. Roger himself was skeptical about the centralization of the network. Over time, mining pools emerged, distributing the power and increasing network security.

Moreover, the opportunities for buying and selling bitcoins were also limited, making it difficult for mainstream users to access the network. Governments and financial institutions initially viewed Bitcoin suspiciously, unsure how to regulate it, creating uncertainty and hampered mainstream adoption. In 2010, while Roger was still rummaging through the novel world of Bitcoin, he came across a whimsical post on Bitcointalk that initially seemed like a prank. It came to light that Hanyecz, a resident of Florida, took to the Bitcointalk forum on May 18, 2010, with an unusual request. He announced his desire to buy two large pizzas using Bitcoin and offered a whopping 10,000 BTC to anyone who would fulfill his pizza order.

The post read, *"I'll pay 10,000 bitcoins for a couple of pizzas... maybe two large ones so I have some leftover for the next day."* It also included, *"You can make the pizza yourself and bring it to my house or order it for me from a delivery place, but what I'm aiming for is getting food delivered in exchange for bitcoins where I don't have to order or prepare it myself."*[25] Hanyecz also mentioned the details of how he would like the pizza for anyone interested in his offer. At that time, the value of Bitcoin was less than half a cent per coin, making the offer seemingly extravagant, while many considered it just a joke. Roger saw the post and people's response to it. Someone asked Hanyecz for his address, while someone else suggested he sell those bitcoins on a trading platform. People from other parts of the world also jumped on it, expressing that they would be interested in the offer if they could see how the payment system would work.

Days went by, and it seemed that Hanyecz's quest for Bitcoin-powered pizzas would go unfulfilled. On May 21, 2010, as Roger checked the discussion, he found another comment from Hanyecz asking, *"So nobody wants to buy me a pizza? Is the Bitcoin amount I'm offering too low?"* A day later, on May 22, 2010, a fellow forum user named Jeremy Sturdivant, who went by the username "Jercos," stepped up to the challenge. Sturdivant agreed to order and deliver the pizzas to Hanyecz in exchange for 10,000 BTC. Catering to the requirement, Hanyecz mentioned that the user got the pizzas delivered to Hanyecz from Papa John's.

So, someone finally bought this man his pizzas in exchange for BTC. Roger thought it seemed like people had developed their trust around it while reading Hanyecz's comment about thanking the user, Jercos, for fulfilling his wish. For crypto enthusiasts like Roger, it was a breakthrough in the cryptocurrency ecosystem.

On June 12, 2010, Roger came across Hanyecz's comment again, where he mentioned keeping the offer open for anyone interested. However, a few months later, he informed the users about holding off on the offer since he couldn't generate thousands of coins daily. At the same time, his "pizzas for Bitcoin" challenge kept gaining massive popularity. At that time, no one knew that the legendary transaction would prove to be a turning point for the cryptocurrency market. Roger, however, found the transaction interesting. "The first documented use of Bitcoin to buy physical goods would definitely go down in history as an important event," he anticipated.

The upcoming time proved the accuracy of Roger's anticipation as the transaction that proved to be the first tangible use case of digital currency served as a landmark, helping people believe in the legitimacy of digital currency. In the same year, another person named Gavin Andresen, the chief developer of the open-source code that defined the rules of the Bitcoin network, gained massive popularity in the infant Bitcoin world when he made a website called "The Bitcoin Faucet." Roger visited the website out of curiosity, and what he found out seemed unbelievable to him. As he accessed the web page, it showed a free Bitcoin giveaway offer for just solving a captcha.

"I'm giving away five bitcoins per visitor; just solve the 'captcha,' then enter your Bitcoin receiving address and press get some." (A Bitcoin faucet is used to initially receive a small amount of bitcoins into a newly created wallet to pay for the transaction cost or network fees (gas) to send bitcoins to another wallet address.)

"Really? Is this a prank or something?" Roger thought while going through the website.

"Doesn't really seem like a prank. Well, it doesn't hurt trying it out, I guess," he said to himself and solved the easy captcha that only took a few seconds to validate. He followed the other instructions and was surprised to see five bitcoins transferred to his account.

"This will help me send and receive bitcoins in the new wallet I created on Bitcoin Core (full node)," he said, not realizing how those five bitcoins would help him later in his life. The website remained operational for the next two years and donated around 19,700 bitcoins to the website visitors.

By 2010, as people's interest grew even more and different ways of obtaining Bitcoin began surfacing, Bitcoin exchanges emerged. Roger was excited to see the development in the

Bitcoin world that seemed to make the digital currency accessible to ordinary users. Around the same time, Roger found a post on Bitcointalk about the proposed idea of establishing a Bitcoin exchange in progress. Someone wrote, *"I'm in the process of building an exchange. I have big plans for it, but I still have a lot of work to do. It will be a real market where people will be able to buy and sell bitcoins with each other."* Other programmers showed interest, and the user who had generated the idea shared the progress with others. With gradual developments, the exchange platform launched the same year. It worked like any other exchange where buyers could purchase Bitcoins against their fiat money. The buyers would hold the Bitcoins in an escrow account till the time sellers received their money. The buyers could purchase Bitcoins in exchange for U.S. dollars transferred through a platform like PayPal.

By the end of 2010, Satoshi Nakamoto, the mastermind behind the Bitcoin saga, posted a message on Bitcointalk saying, *"There's more work to do on DoS, but I'm doing a quick build of what I have so far, in case it's needed, before venturing into more complex ideas."* The message contained some other details, too, but neither Roger nor other users knew that it was Satoshi's last public message before disappearing into thin air by April 2011. Before he cut communication with the world, it was estimated that around one-quarter of the total 21 million bitcoins were generated. One day, while surfing the web, Roger came across a more organized exchange called Mt. Gox, which was referred to as the first-ever Bitcoin exchange. At one point, Mt. Gox was a

Japan-based Bitcoin exchange that was the world's largest cryptocurrency exchange, handling a significant percentage of all Bitcoin transactions.

"What's this name driven from? Mt. Gox... Sounds interesting. Let me see what it stands for," Roger said while exploring the details of the platform. He discovered that the acronym "Mt. Gox" stands for "Magic: The Gathering Online Exchange." Going into more detail reveals that the domain was initially acquired in 2007 to facilitate the trading of cards for the popular "Magic: The Gathering" card game.

However, after learning about Bitcoin in 2010, the owner realized the need for a Bitcoin exchange and converted the platform into a cryptocurrency exchange. The more Roger delved into it, the more his curiosity increased. He learned that the platform was founded in 2010 by Jed McCaleb, who later sold it to Mark Karpeles in March 2011.

Under Karpeles' ownership, the platform transitioned to a Bitcoin exchange. Mt. Gox quickly became the leading Bitcoin exchange, handling the majority of Bitcoin transactions worldwide. At its peak, it was estimated to be handling around 70-80% of all Bitcoin transactions.

In 2011, many other Bitcoin exchanges also surfaced, and that's when the infamous Mt. Gox's fallout began, marked by security breaches and financial difficulties. Mt. Gox faced several security breaches over the years. In June 2011, the exchange suffered a significant hack that led to the theft of thousands of

Bitcoins. Despite this, the platform continued operations. It all started when a platform, VirWox, began facilitating trades between Linden Dollars (the virtual currency of the famous game Second Life) and Bitcoins. Another platform, Tradehill, another Bitcoin exchange launched in 2011, facilitated the instant purchase of Bitcoin without the condition of submitting limit orders on the exchanges. Soon after McCaleb sold the platform to Karpeles, a hacker attacked and sold a Mt. Gox account with a significant number of Bitcoins, leading to a considerable drop in Bitcoin's value. The currency's value dipped from $17 to $0 within a few minutes.

Additionally, the hacker stole some other information on the platform, eventually forcing the site to go offline and cease its operations. Despite the temporary shutdown, only two years later, the site reemerged, handling around 70% of the Bitcoin trade. In 2013, Mt. Gox experienced severe technical issues and halted withdrawals for its users. The exchange claimed it was due to a bug in the Bitcoin software, but suspicions arose about financial mismanagement and potential insolvency. The following year, 2014, started with the company dominating a significant part of the global Bitcoin trade; however, by the end of the second month, the company had filed for bankruptcy protection.

Roger couldn't forget the day when he suddenly found out about the company filing for bankruptcy. On February 7, 2014, the company restricted all Bitcoin withdrawals, claiming the restriction to be a temporary pause for a clear, technical view of the currency process. Later on, on February 24, 2014, the company suspended all trading operations and made the website go offline. All the users lost access to their accounts and assets in the blink of an eye. Although the assets weren't lost, they were frozen for the users, and they lost access to them for the upcoming years. It was later found that the number of Bitcoins lost accounted for around 740,000 and, according to some sources, 850,000.[26] That accounted for around 6% of the total Bitcoins existent at that time.

Additionally, a significant amount of around $27 million was found missing from the company's account, leading to a significant financial and goodwill loss. It was reported that, eventually, 200,000 bitcoins were recovered. However, the remaining 650,000 remained unaccounted for. On February 28, 2014, Mt. Gox filed for bankruptcy protection in Japan, stating that it had lost 850,000 Bitcoins (worth approximately $450 million at that time) in a hacking attack. The bankruptcy filing revealed that the exchange had liabilities exceeding its assets.

As a result of the happenings, Mark Karpeles faced legal action in Japan, accused of embezzlement and falsifying financial records. He denied any wrongdoing and claimed the missing Bitcoins were the result of hacking. Investigations into the Mt. Gox collapse continued, with authorities looking into the circumstances surrounding the loss of Bitcoins and potential negligence on the part of the exchange's management. The collapse of Mt. Gox significantly impacted the perception of cryptocurrency exchanges and highlighted the importance of security, transparency, and regulatory compliance in the cryptocurrency industry. It also led to increased efforts to establish regulatory frameworks for cryptocurrency exchanges globally. Roger, however, never lost belief in the digital currency and reckoned its potential to transform the existing financial systems. Instead, he perceived the collapse of Mt. Gox with a different approach. He believed that the creation of Mt. Gox and other early cryptocurrency exchanges marked the evolution of the crypto landscape.

These platforms provided the infrastructure needed for enthusiasts, early adopters, and investors to participate in the burgeoning Bitcoin ecosystem. While the early exchanges faced challenges, they laid the groundwork for the robust and diverse cryptocurrency exchange landscape seen today, contributing to the ongoing growth and development of the digital asset market.

During the peaks and valleys of Mt. Gox, Roger came across Silk Road—the dark web marketplace using Bitcoin as the means of exchange.

Famously regarded as the first dark web online marketplace, The Silk Road was an online dark web marketplace known for facilitating illegal transactions, primarily involving the buying and selling of illicit drugs and other goods. The Silk Road operated as a hidden service on the Tor Network as a part of the dark web. Roger searched the term "dark web" on Google, and the results showed that the *"dark web is a part of the internet that lets people hide their identity and location from other people and law enforcement."*[27] Going more into the details revealed that the dark web is a portion of the internet that is intentionally hidden and only accessible through specific software, most commonly the Tor (The Onion Router) network.

The Tor network is an open-source platform that masks online traffic, creating anonymity for users who browse different websites and access servers. Users on the dark web often remain anonymous by using specialized software like Tor. Tor directs internet traffic through a series of volunteer-operated servers operated globally to conceal a user's location (or spoof), IP address, and browser history, all of which are encrypted from network surveillance or traffic analysis. Tor's "onion routing" encrypts data in layers, like the layers of an onion, making it difficult to trace the origin of the communication, helping to provide anonymity to both users and websites on the dark web. The use of the dark web is controversial since it is infamous for illegal activities.

Since the use of fiat currency and conventional payment platforms gave regulators access to transaction information, facilitating their ability to trace and catch perpetrators, the payment of choice quickly became bitcoin, driving demand for users to obtain the coins.

The creation of a functional marketplace for cryptocurrency and Bitcoin was in demand. The Silk Road became a pioneer in offering Bitcoin one of its first use cases for anonymized stores of value to transact between buyers and sellers of goods. Operated by Ross Ulbricht under the pseudonym "Dread Pirate Roberts," the Silk Road became infamous for its role in the underground economy. Ross Ulbricht launched the Silk Road in 2011 as a Tor hidden service, providing users with a platform for anonymous marketplace transactions. The marketplace gained popularity for its user-friendly interface and the ability to conduct transactions beyond the reach of traditional law enforcement.

Due to its unique model, the Silk Road quickly became a hub for illegal activities, including drug trafficking, counterfeit currency sales, hacking tools, and more. Cryptocurrencies, particularly Bitcoin, were the primary medium of exchange since the Bitcoin whitepaper defined its privacy features as *"the public can see that someone is sending an amount to someone, but without information, linking the transaction to anyone."*[28] As the Silk Road gained notoriety, law enforcement agencies, including the FBI, initiated investigations to identify and apprehend those involved in running the marketplace. The anonymity provided by Tor and cryptocurrencies posed challenges for authorities. The Silk Road case drew attention to the use of cryptocurrencies for illegal activities, leading to concerns about their potential misuse. It also prompted discussions about the need for regulatory frameworks and law enforcement capabilities in the digital asset space.

As a result of interrogations and actions against the underground drug market, the FBI cracked down on the illegal drug market, arresting the accused culprits, permanently terminating the site, and seizing around 144,000 bitcoins ($8.6b in 2024). The Silk Road case had far-reaching implications, influencing public perception, regulatory discussions, and law enforcement strategies in the cryptocurrency ecosystem. It underscored the challenges associated with anonymity in online transactions and highlighted the importance of balancing privacy with security in the evolving digital landscape.

Among the early adopters, like Roger and Hanyecz, was Charlie Shrem, a young college graduate in Economics and Finance who was a college student when Bitcoin emerged. Born to Jewish parents, he always aimed to become a rabbi. However, fate had different plans for him. Seeing the potential in the cryptocurrency, Shrem began investing in Bitcoin. However, his journey didn't prove to be a smooth road, as he lost the stake as a result of a crash in his storage service. The loss didn't turn his feelings bitter towards the digital currency. Instead, he drew inspiration from it and launched BitInstant, a platform helping users convert their fiat money into cryptocurrency. Over time, BitInstant proved to be a massive success, and at one point, accounting for around 30% of all Bitcoin transactions. The company's notable performance gained enormous attention from people, attracting various investors. Amidst the surging popularity of BitInstant, Charlie Shrem described himself as a "Bitcoin Purist."

As a strong and vocal supporter of digital currencies, particularly Bitcoin, Charlie Shrem experienced a soaring increase in his wealth. Then came a dark phase in Charlie Shrem's sparkling life and career when he was imprisoned for two years in 2014. During the Silk Road case, Shrem was accused of his indirect involvement in a massive transaction of around a million dollars in bitcoin on a black market exchange. The serious allegations led him to a sentence of two years in jail. The investigative reports revealed that the incident happened back in 2012 when Shrem facilitated Robert Faiella in carrying out a Bitcoin transaction on the Silk Road. As Fiella pleaded guilty, Shrem was caught under investigation, later officially pleading guilty in 2014. The multiple litigations and the penalties caused Shrem to lose nearly all of his money.

After his release from prison, Shrem continued to be a strong advocate of digital currencies and Bitcoin. Roger's story was even more enjoyable.

The exploration of the Silk Road case led Roger to himself in the study of Charlie Shrem, Roger, and other early adopters of Bitcoin and cryptocurrency. Despite dreaming of becoming a garbage truck driver in his childhood, Roger was destined to explore the world of cryptocurrency and gain massive popularity in the cryptocurrency ecosystem, which gave him the name of "Bitcoin Jesus."

He came to notice it when he purchased Baklava for 14 BTC from another early Bitcoin adopter named Mandrick. However, he discovered Bitcoin back in 2011 and called it "one of the most important inventions in the history of humankind. When Bitcoin was valued under $1 in the early days, Roger realized its potential and collected an estimated 400,000 BTC. However, later, his collection was reduced in the process of spreading the word about cryptocurrency among the public and financially supporting the launch of various Bitcoin startups. He even became an early investor in the company BitInstant, founded by Charlie Shrem. The year 2013 saw the price of Bitcoin rising for the first time, reaching $1,000. "That's massive," Roger thought while watching the news. His mind went towards the 5 BTCs that he had gained from the "Bitcoin Faucet" website.

However, the price hike didn't pass the test of time and quickly dipped. Roger recalled what the CEO of Euro Pacific Capital, Peter Schiff, had said about the extraordinary hike in BTC value. He said, "A bubble is a bubble. And there's a bubble in Bitcoin." The people who had invested in Bitcoin, seeing the massive price hike and anticipating the growth trend to continue, lost a considerable amount of their investments. Not only did the early adopters lose a substantial amount of money, but public opinion about digital currency and Bitcoins also witnessed some negative trends. However, the sudden price hike and then the price drop proved to be a significant milestone in the journey of Bitcoin's growth. That was the time when Roger saw many people talking and learning about cryptocurrency. Some were even buying some bitcoins after hearing about it for the first time. However, Roger realized that this quick price appreciation wasn't the first time in Bitcoin price history. Looking back on the development of Bitcoin, he realized that the currency had witnessed "bubble periods" earlier, too, when the price of Bitcoin hiked and then dropped sharply.

The first one was in February 2011, when BTC equaled $1.06. The time was later called the Great Slashdotting or the Dollar Parity Day. It all happened when Bitcoin was mentioned on the news aggregator platform Slashdot and drove the interest of prominent tech experts and enthusiasts like McCaleb and Jeff Garzik. The increasing interest then drove the value of the Bitcoin high, meeting one dollar for the first time. However, the sharp increase was soon followed by a sudden decline in value on April 5, 2011, when one BTC was valued at $0.67. Later in the same year, in June, Bitcoin witnessed a wild bubble when an article was published about the potential of cryptocurrency to purchase illegal drugs and items on "dark web" websites such as the Silk Road.

The revelations and claims made in the article, combined with the Bitcoin exchanges facilitating the purchase of tokens, led to a massive increase in the value of Bitcoin from $10 to $30. Just like the previous time, the upcoming months brought a decline in the value that settled at $2.14. The third bubble was the thousandaire when the 2013 BTC reached $1,000. Although the prices later dropped, they still maintained increased price action for a little longer, finally settling at $172.15 in January 2015.

"It was indeed a bumpy ride, but the results are inevitable. Each time the bubble crashed, the price of Bitcoin settled at a higher point than the previous low," Roger exclaimed as he recalled the ups and downs of Bitcoin's journey to gain value.

Considering the perceived privacy shortcomings of Bitcoin, Monero (XMR) was introduced in 2014 as a cryptocurrency that strongly emphasizes privacy and anonymity. Monero's primary objective is to provide users with enhanced fungibility, privacy, and security in their financial transactions. The currency uses a technology called ring signatures to obfuscate the source of transactions. In a typical cryptocurrency transaction, the sender's identity is linked to the transaction. With ring signatures, multiple public keys, including the sender's, are used to create a ring of possible signers, making it difficult to determine which specific key initiated the transaction. Since the emergence of Monero in 2014, it has become a popular choice among dark web users because of its foolproof privacy protection feature.

Another development that strengthened Roger's belief in Bitcoin was when, in 2013, Reddit began accepting payments in Bitcoin for an enhanced membership.

A huge development in the same year was when a US court declared that Bitcoin was a form of currency or money.[29] Roger considered that judgment to be historical in defining the worth of Bitcoin and paving the way for its future growth. In the same year, the first Bitcoin ATM was installed in a coffee shop in Vancouver.[30] Roger knew that the horizons for the growth of this transformative currency were limitless and that he must not refrain from playing his role in the growth and development of Bitcoin.

He understood that the impact of Bitcoin's value increase on early investors was profound, marking a significant turning point in their financial portfolios.

Early adopters, including visionaries like Roger and Charlie Shrem, witnessed substantial returns on their investments as Bitcoin's value surged over time. When the price was minimal, those who recognized its potential in the nascent stages experienced exponential growth in the value of their holdings. The decentralized nature of Bitcoin allowed early investors to benefit from its scarcity, as the fixed supply of 21 million coins contributed to increased demand. As more individuals and institutional investors recognized the transformative potential of cryptocurrency, the market witnessed a surge in demand, leading to a substantial increase in Bitcoin's price.

The impact on early investors extended beyond financial gains. They played a crucial role in shaping the narrative around Bitcoin, advocating for its adoption and dispelling skepticism. As Bitcoin gained mainstream attention and acceptance, the early investors were at the forefront of a financial revolution.

Contemplating the factors leading to the growth of Bitcoin, Roger concluded that the growing acceptance and adoption of Bitcoin as a legitimate form of investment and means of payment played a crucial role. With more businesses and individuals accepting Bitcoin, its value and usage increased in everyday transactions.

Moreover, since Bitcoin has a capped supply of 21 million coins, this scarcity and rising demand tend to drive up the price. The involvement of institutional investors and large corporations in the cryptocurrency space provided validation and legitimacy to Bitcoin. Lastly, he believed that the growing public awareness and understanding of Bitcoin contributed to increased trust and adoption. As more people become familiar with the technology and its potential, the demand for Bitcoin as a decentralized, borderless money and store of value rose. Considering the immense potential and growth of Bitcoin, Roger was ready to dive into Bitcoin mining and realize its true potential.

Chapter 3: The Development of Cryptocurrency

Amidst the value fluctuations and other events in the cryptocurrency ecosystem, what never changed was the development of cryptocurrency. As Roger dived into the world of Bitcoin mining, he realized that some other cryptocurrencies had become a part of the crypto ecosystem and were known as altcoins. As Bitcoin gained momentum and captured the world's attention with its revolutionary blockchain technology, it paved the way for the emergence of a diverse ecosystem of cryptocurrencies. These digital assets, collectively known as altcoins, began to proliferate, each offering its unique features, use cases, and innovations.

Upon inquiring about the term, Roger found out that *"every cryptocurrency that is not the original Bitcoin is considered an alternative to it, hence an alternative coin or altcoin."*[31]

"Oh, so an altcoin is any cryptocurrency that is not Bitcoin," Roger exclaimed. The introduction of alternative cryptocurrencies presaged that people had begun trusting the idea of the cryptocurrencies as Roger had anticipated. His confidence in the potential of cryptocurrency strengthened even more.

The year 2011, when the Bitcoin value experienced its first bubble, significantly increased its popularity and drew people towards the idea of bitcoins. That was the same year when several rival cryptocurrencies came into existence. The popular platform Bitcointalk.org became one of Roger's go-to platforms for staying updated about the latest developments in the ecosystem. On October 9, 2011, a catchy headline caught Roger's attention as he saw a post with the title *"Litecoin—a lite version of Bitcoin. Launched!"*[32]

"This looks interesting," Roger exclaimed as he began reading the post, his pupils widening as his brain registered the information he skimmed from the post. It mentioned, *"Litecoin is the result of some of us who joined together on IRC to create a real alternative currency similar to Bitcoin. We wanted to make a coin that is silver to Bitcoin's gold."*

It also highlighted some of the other alternative coins that were launched along with their downsides and then explained how Litecoin could solve the problems other coins had. The coin was based on the latest Bitcoin code, and the author mentioned, *"We have come up with a plan that we believe is the most fair. Some previous coins were released without Windows binaries or without source code; we consider this as unfair as it is unsafe. We released the source code and binaries ahead of time... three days before launch."*

After a poll was conducted about the launch time, Litecoin was launched on October 12, 2011, and gained massive traction. Former Google engineer Charlie Lee created the coin, and speculations suggested that the coin aimed to improve upon Bitcoin's shortcomings, offering faster transaction times and a different hashing algorithm. Roger began mining Litecoins to verify the authenticity of the claims made in the Bitcointalk.org discussion. After following up with Litecoin, he realized that, as promised, Litecoin significantly reduced the block construction time from 10 to 2.5 minutes. It had a coin minting limit of 84 million coins compared to the 21 million limit for Bitcoin, and the halving occurred every 840,000 blocks.[33] However, the claim that *"We wanted the best innovation of Bitcoin and these other currencies to create a coin with all of their benefits, but nearly none of their problems"* wasn't entirely valid. Litecoin had some challenges halting its efficiency and blocking its way to becoming the best alternative to Bitcoin. The time reduction led to a range of challenges and efficiency issues. One of them was an increase in the number of orphaned blocks—any block that is not in the main chain after a temporary ledger conflict.[34]

Orphaned blocks are the legitimate blocks whose parent blocks are either non-existent or unknown. Although the block is valid and solved within the blockchain network, it is not accepted by the network because another valid block is being added to the network at the same time. In the same year, some other altcoins, such as Namecoin and Swiftcoin, were also introduced. Just like Litecoin, other altcoins offered incremental improvements to the original Bitcoin protocol. The following year, in November 2012, the first halving of Bitcoin occurred, marking a significant event in Bitcoin history. Although it initially had no significant impact on Bitcoin's value, the impacts gradually became visible as Bitcoin's value increased steadily the following year. In 2014, another notable altcoin, Monero (XMR), was launched, and it specifically addressed the privacy issues of Bitcoin. Like Litecoin, Monero was also introduced on the Bitcointalk platform with a post stating, *"Bitmonero, a new coin based on CryptoNote technology, launched."*[35] Launched as a privacy-focused cryptocurrency, Monero offered enhanced anonymity features compared to Bitcoin. Its implementation of ring signatures and stealth addresses aimed to provide users with greater privacy and fungibility, addressing concerns about the traceability of transactions on the Bitcoin blockchain. By that time, Brian Armstrong and Fred Ehrsam had launched Coinbase, the world's most recognized cryptocurrency exchange.

A year later, the Ethereum project was launched after the fall of Mt. Gox in 2015. By then, Roger had become quite adept at understanding cryptocurrencies' functions. Another notable development was the launch of Ethereum in 2015.[36] The Russian-Canadian programmer Vitalik Buterin created it in 2013. However, he didn't launch the Ethereum blockchain until 2015. Ethereum took the concept of blockchain technology a step further by enabling the development of decentralized applications (DApps) and smart contracts. Its flexible and programmable blockchain sparked a wave of innovation, creating a wide range of tokens and projects built on its platform.

Roger considered the launch of Ethereum to be the first truly valuable implementation of the ideas working behind Bitcoin.

"This launch seems to bring a breakthrough in the world of cryptocurrency," Roger thought as he found out about smart contracts, a technology allowing the blockchain to host software applications on it while also facilitating crypto transactions. The validators adding blocks to the blockchain in a proof of stake system using the Ethereum protocol/blockchain received Ether (ETH), the cryptocurrency. Roger saw people using the terms Ether and Ethereum interchangeably in the crypt world; however, he knew the difference between the two.

Upon examining different altcoins, Roger found out that the key benefits they offered over Bitcoin were higher speed, enhanced anonymity, and easier access. The proliferation of altcoins gave rise to various token standards and categories. Roger discovered that the altcoins being introduced varied greatly in their nature and functionality. The most popular of them included utility tokens, stablecoins, and security tokens.

Utility tokens are digital assets that provide access to a product or service within a specific blockchain ecosystem. "Let's get into more details," Roger said, looking for a more comprehensive and meaningful definition. He discovered that they *"refer to blockchain-based tokens that have a specific use and offer utility. They are created on a blockchain and are native to the platform they are created on."[37]* They are often issued during Initial Coin Offerings (ICOs) or Token Generation Events (TGEs) and represent a form of digital asset ownership. Utility tokens can grant holders rights or privileges within a decentralized application (DApp) or platform, such as voting rights, access to premium features, or discounts on services. "Oh, so Ethereum's Ether (ETH) is a utility token, which fuels transactions on the Ethereum network and is used to pay for gas fees when executing smart contracts," Roger's eyes sparked as he grasped the concept of utility tokens. He then explored the other types of altcoins.

Stablecoins, as the name refers, is an altcoin that is intended to offer price stability compared to Bitcoin. To understand it more clearly, Roger looked for other sources. He found that *"A stablecoin is a cryptocurrency that aims to maintain price stability by pegging its monetary value to a given fiat currency, typically on a one-to-one basis."*[38] Since the value of a stable asset is backed by its market value, it facilitates price stability, something that doesn't exist in bitcoins. Unlike other cryptocurrencies, stablecoins aim to mitigate the volatility of digital assets, making them suitable for everyday transactions, remittances, and hedging strategies.

Roger also found out that stablecoins can be pegged to fiat currencies like the US dollar (USD), commodities like gold, or other cryptocurrencies. They provide stability and liquidity to cryptocurrency markets and bridge traditional finance and the decentralized economy. Upon his search for the best stablecoins, the names of Tether (USDT), USD Coin (USDC), and Dai (DAI) topped the lists.

Lastly, he explored security tokens, understanding that *"a security token is a cryptographic token that is tied to a securities offering."*[39] Security tokens represent ownership of an underlying asset, similar to traditional securities like stocks, bonds, or real estate. Unlike utility tokens, security tokens are subject to regulatory oversight as they typically derive their value from external, tradable assets. These tokens are often issued through Security Token Offerings (STOs) and provide investors with the potential for financial returns based on the underlying asset's performance.

"So, the security tokens are a kind of equity shared by the blockchain companies," Roger summarized the information for a quick and better understanding. Over time, other types of altcoins, such as meme coins, governance tokens, and play-to-earn tokens, emerged and gained attention.

The meme coins, particularly Dogecoin, the flagship of meme coins, became significantly popular. What surprised Roger most about their popularity was that those coins were initially created as a joke. Dogecoin, *"the accidental crypto movement that makes people smile,"*[40] was created by IBM software engineer Billy Marcus and Adobe software engineer Jackson Palmer and launched in December 2013. Although meme coins gained public attention, their low per-unit price due to high supply limited their adoption among investors.

Over time, Roger's interest in the cryptocurrency world kept increasing as he began mining different coins, including Bitcoin. He recalled July 31, 2013, when he was scouring through the Bitcointalk forum and came across the post of a guy named J.R. Willett. It said, *"I am very excited to announce that I now have a complete specification for building a protocol layer on top of Bitcoin (like how HTTP runs on top of TCP/IP)."*[41]

The author named the new protocol layer "MasterCoin" and claimed to have invented and published that name before the introduction of the altcoin of the same name. The post also revealed that *The coins of the new layer have,*

- *Additional security features to make your money much harder to steal.*

- *Built-in support for a distributed currency exchange.*

- *Built-in support for distributed betting (no need to trust a website to coordinate bets)*

- *Built-in support for "smart property" can be used to create and transfer property such as titles, deeds, or stock in a company.*

- *Capability to hold a stable user-defined value, such as an ounce of gold or a US dollar, with no need to trust a person promising to back up that value.*

The post also said that the *"MasterCoins are intended to be an investment opportunity on par with buying bitcoins when they first came out."*

"So, this is kind of a fundraising proposal, and the guy must be intending to fund his idea," Roger deduced after reading the complete thread. His analysis was accurate as Willet began asking for some BTC donations. To keep the investors motivated, he revealed, "Once you own MasterCoins, you have the building blocks for creating GoldCoin, USDCoin, EuroCoin, and any other real-world asset you can imagine."[42] Roger read the document and analyzed the risks of investing in MasterCoin, as explained by Willett. One of which said, *"MasterCoins are an experimental currency, built on another experimental currency (bitcoin). The risks and potential rewards are extreme."* Roger kept following up on the thread to track the progress and found out that the proposal received a massive response from the people in August; approximately 4740 BTC worth ($500K at the time) was raised. The fundraiser was known as the first ICO (Initial Coin Offering), where BTCs were sent to the "Exodus Address," leading to the creation of MasterCoins. The "Exodus Address" was similar to the Bitcoin blockchain, Genesis Block, which led to the creation of Bitcoin.

Upon researching ICOs, Roger discovered that *"In an ICO, a startup creates and distributes its "digital tokens" typically in exchange for Bitcoin, Ethereum, or fiat currencies (E.g., US dollars) to raise capital to fund their operations."*[43]

Initial Coin Offerings (ICOs) were launched as a means of crowdfunding. Similar to an IPO (Initial Public Offering), where a company lists its stocks for the general public to purchase to collect funds, ICOs were also a form of fundraising.

In these offerings, cryptocurrencies were offered in the form of tokens to the investors in return for their bitcoins. The investors can hold the tokens, anticipating the project to be successful and the value of the tokens to increase and yield worthwhile returns to the investors. Unlike IPOs, where the investors get security tokens to receive dividend rights, ICOs offer utility tokens where the investors have the right to use the products. *"Utility tokens are tokens which are intended to provide digital access to an application or service."*[44]

After studying various ICOs and their operations, Roger understood that the primary purpose of ICOs was to raise funds for the development and implementation of blockchain-based projects. The projects included decentralized applications (DApps), platforms, protocols, and digital assets. These projects aimed to address various industry challenges, innovate existing processes, and create new decentralized solutions across different sectors in the industry.

Over time, he observed that ICO tokens served multiple purposes within the project's ecosystem. Besides the primary function of fundraising, ICO tokens provide holders with access to specific products, services, or functionalities. They also offered investors the opportunity to invest in early-stage blockchain projects and benefit from the anticipated success of the project. Although the projects' success wasn't guaranteed, investors could participate in ICOs with the anticipation of value appreciation and potential ROIs.

People believed that the years after 2015 brought a flood of ICOs. However, Roger thought that the concept of ICOs had come into view quite earlier. He recalled his memories of 2013 when he heard about MasterCoin and some other similar projects that did precisely what ICOs referred to. Roger felt that the development of the cryptocurrency market had been greatly influenced by initial coin offerings (ICOs), which provide startups and blockchain-based ventures with a novel way to raise money.

ICOs emerged as a popular method for entrepreneurs and developers to raise capital by issuing digital tokens to investors in exchange for cryptocurrency contributions, typically Bitcoin (BTC) or Ethereum (ETH). The tokens issued during ICOs represent a form of digital asset ownership and often grant holders access to a project's products, services, or ecosystem.

In his opinion, ICOs democratized access to capital, allowing innovative projects and startups to raise funds directly from a global pool of investors without relying on traditional financial intermediaries like banks or venture capitalists. The decentralized fundraising model empowered entrepreneurs to pursue their ideas and initiatives, fostering creativity, innovation, and competition within the blockchain space. They also facilitated the launch of a diverse range of projects, including decentralized applications (DApps), blockchain platforms, digital currencies, and utility tokens for various industries.

The developments in the cryptocurrency ecosystem proved that ICOs paved the way for the tokenization of real-world assets. This development enabled the representation of physical or digital assets as blockchain-based tokens. As a result, investors could have fractional ownership with enhanced transferability and liquidity of traditionally non-liquid assets. As ICOs allowed companies to tokenize assets such as real estate or company equity, they provided investors with new investment opportunities and asset classes previously unavailable in traditional markets.

The flood of ICOs included various legitimate offerings; however, they weren't completely protected from "get rich quick" schemes, and some others were only scammed offerings. The emergence of cryptocurrencies and initial coin offerings (ICOs) gave rise to debates concerning the laws governing these entities. Initial Coin Offerings (ICOs) have gained popularity as a means of collecting cash for projects by selling tokens to investors. However, market integrity and investor protection have been questioned due to the absence of governmental oversight and the increase in fraud schemes.

One of the scams that gained the most traction among others was a "pump and dump" scheme. The scheme was built around the principles of supply and demand, where people began intentionally pumping cryptocurrencies into the market by purchasing large quantities early on launch or creation. Coin or contract authors then made massive buys, which rapidly pushed up the price and increased speculation and fear of missing out (FOMO) among retail buyers. Once the value of the coin topped out, the contract maker would remove liquidity or sell/dump the coin at the highest price, which only benefitted the contract creator or early whales of the coin.

The in-depth research of the pump and dump schemes revealed that *"P&D is a form of price manipulation that involves artificially inflating an asset price before selling the cheaply purchased asset at a higher price. Once the assets are dumped, the price falls, and the investors lose money."*[45]

Roger invested a significant amount of his time and efforts in studying P&D schemes and found some ways to identify such schemes to avoid falling victim to them. He realized that to identify such schemes, he must be aware of the unusual market trends, such as a sudden surge in the purchase of a particular cryptocurrency without any reasonable factors justifying the surging demand. Moreover, avoiding letting emotions take control when making the investment decision was crucial to avoid buying tokens with susceptible backgrounds or bad/exploitable code. Nevertheless, investing in cryptocurrencies with a reliable structure and backed by credible personalities could also be a way to avoid scams. Roger decided to incorporate these tips to reduce the risk of getting scammed since he wasn't the type to leave a viable and promising-looking currency because of mere risks and controversies.

Besides the pump-and-dump scheme, other controversies and regulatory issues also surrounded ICOs, and regulators worldwide began scrutinizing these fundraising events to address potential risks. One of the primary concerns surrounding ICOs that Roger identified was the lack of investor protection mechanisms compared to traditional investment vehicles.

Since ICOs' operation differed from traditional securities offerings, they left investors vulnerable to fraudulent schemes, scams, and market manipulation. Moreover, market manipulation tactics like insider trading and price manipulation also posed systematic risks to the ecosystem and undermined investor confidence. Initially, the ICO landscape wasn't regulated, creating user uncertainty. In 2017, a year after the second Bitcoin halving happened, Roger found himself surrounded by a multitude of cryptocurrencies, competing with the existing currencies and aiming to become the best alternative to Bitcoin.

Ether, the highly liquid cryptocurrency of Ethereum's blockchain 2.0, gained the most attention. Although the coin supply of Ether wasn't limited, its founder, Vialik Buterin, revealed that the supply of the coins would not reach more than 100,000,000 ETH in the foreseeable future.[46]

"Do you really think that Ether can steal Bitcoin's thunder this year?" Roger asked one of his friends, who was also a cryptocurrency enthusiast like Roger.

"Do you remember when Ethereum raised money through ICO in 2014?" his friend asked.

"Of course; how can I forget that it raised around 31,000 BTC within a few hours back then," Roger replied.

"The number of BTC raised through that ICO speaks volumes of people's trust in this currency," Roger's friend said.

"I agree."

"Now, the platform allows people to trade cryptocurrencies in a way similar to public stocks. Isn't this a breakthrough?" his friend asked, and Roger couldn't agree more.

However, during the upcoming time, he saw the governments raising concerns about the legitimacy and regulation of the Ethereum blockchain, leading China to ban it altogether while the

SEC turned vigilant eyes on Ethereum to trace activities that might have gone unnoticed by the security fringes. "This Bitcoin saga doesn't seem to stop without revolutionizing the existing financial systems, and the world isn't ready to experience the groundbreaking progression awaiting ahead," Roger mumbled while looking out of the window while his computer was glowing with the words, *"$257Million: Filecoin breaks the all-time record for ICO funding."*[47] He then went into the details of the news that had taken the cryptocurrency world by storm. Protocol Labs raised a whopping $245 million within an hour for Filecoin, which became the hot digital coin offering at that time.[48]

Looking ahead, Roger knew that the future of cryptocurrency promised continued innovation and disruption as developers and entrepreneurs exploring new applications and use cases.

As Roger had anticipated, the year 2017 marked a Bitcoin and cryptocurrency boom. With Ethereum facilitating the emergence of decentralized finance (DeFi) and non-fungible tokens (NFTs) to central bank digital currencies (CBDCs) and cross-border payments, cryptocurrency began reshaping the global economy.

The year followed with a hike in the price of Bitcoin, reaching $10,000 for the first time in history. The surging trend didn't stop until the price of Bitcoin briefly touched $20,000 and then suffered the crypto winter—*"times when cryptocurrencies and tokens take a huge, across-the-board hit in value."*[49]

Roger thought there was still more to come. He anticipated that major financial organizations and banks would soon support Bitcoin as a result of their observation of the cryptocurrency's rise. Roger predicted that in the near future, cryptocurrencies would become more widely used and developed.

Chapter 4: The Impact of Cryptocurrency on Traditional Banking

On his way back home from the bank, Roger pondered over a comparison between traditional banks and cryptocurrency. Ever since Bitcoin emerged, Roger had been considering the prospective fixation of the flaws in the existing financial system. Banks are one of the most crucial elements of the financial system by having a monopoly and ultimate control over the monetary supply circulating in the market. Although the outcome of that ultimate control had proven to be a disaster during the financial crisis of 2007, Roger still couldn't see any visible changes or improvements in the system to fix the leading causes of the financial crisis. Cryptocurrencies and blockchain technology offered a beam of hope for transitioning from centralization to a decentralized system. Roger believed that cryptocurrency's emergence and widespread adoption impacted traditional banking in several ways, ultimately disrupting it entirely.

After spending significant time in the cryptocurrency ecosystem, Roger knew that decentralization and eliminating intermediaries were core cryptocurrency principles that challenged traditional financial and banking systems. Unlike traditional centralized systems where a single authority controls transactions, cryptocurrency operates on decentralized networks, typically powered by blockchain technology. The decentralization distributes control across a network of nodes so that no single entity controls the network, making it resistant to censorship and single points of failure. *"Cryptocurrency enables peer-to-peer (P2P) transactions without the need for intermediaries like banks or payment processors."[50]* Users can send digital assets directly to one another across the blockchain network, bypassing traditional financial institutions. Roger had the first-hand experience of sending funds with a Bitcoin wallet address without involving banks or third-party payment processors.

The elimination of intermediaries facilitates faster, more efficient, and cost-effective transactions on the cryptocurrency network. Besides the increase in speed, eliminating intermediaries also allowed users to have greater control over their funds for conducting transactions with lower fees and reduced friction. Roger had himself experienced trading & swapping through decentralized exchanges (DEXs) that allowed users to trade cryptocurrencies directly with one another without relying on centralized exchanges, eliminating the risks associated with the centralized custody of funds. He knew that a long list of reasons and benefits of a cryptocurrency-based payment system proved it to be better than the traditional banking system.

Curious about people's views about cryptocurrency in contrast to the traditional banking system, Roger once again referred to the popular platform 'Bitcointalk.org' to get some insights about public opinion in this regard. He found some interesting user comments supporting the anticipated move of cryptocurrencies fixing, replacing, and improving the traditional banking system. Someone asked about the difference between crypto and traditional banking, and in response, people highlighted what they thought about the crypto banking system.

"There is no one to blacklist you."

"They do not get to tell you whom you can transact with."

"They do not get to limit your access when the next wave of government inflation hits your life savings, and you are watching your purchasing power melt like an ice cream in Harare."

"They cannot force you to transact, save, and live on money, but they have the power to counterfeit on a whim."

"Bitcoin will not close doors when governments tell them to."[51]

Although, at that time, no such thing as crypto banking existed, public opinion proved that people were thinking about it and had strong opinions in favor and against the cryptocurrency payment system. Someone even said, *"In cryptocurrency, you are a bank for your funds."*

When it came to traditional banking, users mentioned it as the leading cause of depression and crashes, often failing to serve the lower classes in proportion to their contribution. Although general public opinion seemed to be a little inclined towards cryptocurrency-backed payment and banking systems, the narrative of the institutions seemed different. Roger noticed an environment of resistance and non-acceptance of cryptocurrencies by traditional banks. Cryptocurrencies represented a disruptive force that threatened the traditional banking model by offering an alternative financial system outside the control of banks and governments. Banks appeared to view cryptocurrencies as a competitive threat to their business model and sought to downplay their significance.

Besides the existence of direct competition, Roger also noticed some other possible reasons for the dislikeness of cryptocurrencies. Cryptocurrencies' decentralized and unregulated nature made them more like a threat to the banking institutions, which considered them an attractive medium for turning black money into white and performing illegitimate activities. Moreover, the removal of intermediaries made it prone to dismantling the financial system and undermining the cycle of trust.

Although Roger considered cryptocurrency to be a source of disrupting and revolutionizing the existing banking system, he still could not overlook the flaws in the system that undermined the potential of cryptocurrencies. During its early years, cryptocurrency faced significant challenges when interacting with the traditional banking system. Those challenges stemmed from the disruptive nature of cryptocurrencies, which posed a threat to the established banking industry.

Traditional banks initially struggled to understand the concept and technology behind cryptocurrencies. Many bankers viewed cryptocurrencies as a fad or a speculative investment rather than a legitimate form of currency or asset. However, as time passed, the persistence and growth of cryptocurrency proved their doubts wrong. Still, the reluctance of banking institutions to adopt cryptocurrencies persisted. The extreme volatility of cryptocurrency prices, especially during the early years, made traditional banks wary of providing banking services to cryptocurrency exchanges and businesses.

The speculative nature of cryptocurrencies raised concerns about financial stability and the potential for losses. Traditional banks were also concerned about the security risks associated with storing and transacting in cryptocurrencies. High-profile hacking incidents and thefts from cryptocurrency exchanges highlighted the vulnerabilities of digital assets and raised doubts about their reliability as a store of value.

Roger realized the lack of attention from regulatory authorities around the world toward the development of clear guidelines and regulations for cryptocurrencies was also a barrier to halting their adoption. The prevalent uncertainty made traditional banks hesitant to engage with cryptocurrency-related businesses and customers due to concerns about compliance and legal risks.

In May 2019, the news channels highlighted cryptocurrency mixers or tumblers being traced down and terminated by the governments. Upon investigation, he found out that in the cryptocurrency world, a tumbler refers to a *"mixing service that makes cryptocurrency transactions more anonymous by breaking them down into smaller parts and mixing them with others."*[52]

"How does a cryptocurrency tumbler work?" Roger asked one of his friends who worked at a news agency and was covering the news about cryptocurrency tumblers.

"Just like a mixer," he replied.

"What does it mean?" Roger asked, still puzzled about the framework.

"Well, understand it like a pool of money where you and other users dump your cryptocurrencies. The service will then process & mix your funds, then return you the same amount of your cryptocurrency after deducting their service fee," he explained when Roger interrupted.

"What difference does it make if I'm getting the same thing back?" He asked.

"Well, here's the catch. The funds you receive will have originated from many smaller transactions deposited by other users in the system in an attempt to conceal the origins of the original fund's wallet address."

"Oh, I understand now."

"Hence, you get enhanced anonymity since there forms a barrier between the addresses that send and receive the funds," his friend concluded, making him understand the concept of cryptocurrency mixers.

Earlier, Roger used to think about why people needed enhanced anonymity when cryptocurrency provided this feature. However, after years of understanding and using it, he realized that cryptocurrencies offer pseudonymity rather than anonymity. Although they eliminate the need for an intermediary and allow the sender and receiver to transact among themselves without revealing their identity to third parties, the transaction is visible to other users on the blockchain. This meant that anyone on the blockchain using careful blockchain forensics could trace the real identities of the sender and receiver. Therefore, people requiring complete anonymity felt the need for a solution to help them make their transactions entirely unidentified. The creation of mixing services and tumblers was a part of the realization of the need. Even the privacy coins either used high-anonymity consensus protocols or mixers to ensure the highest levels of obfuscation of transaction details. However, the governments eyed cryptocurrency mixers as inappropriate, fearing their use for illegal activities such as money laundering. Considering the threat of strict action from the government authorities, Vitalik Buterin, the co-founder of Ethereum, suggested the creation of an on-chain, smart contract-based Ether mixer to enhance users' privacy on the platform. Roger understood the significance of enhanced anonymity for ensuring the confidentiality of users' data. However, he also knew that the concept of total obfuscation didn't go down well with governing bodies due to the alleged use of that feature for illegal activities.

The government's crackdown against cryptocurrency tumblers received a mixed response from the public. However, cryptocurrency enthusiasts, early adopters, and investors considered it against the growth and development of the industry in the long run. The British-American businessman John McAfee shared his views on Twitter (Now X), stating, *"Bitcoin mixers are now being targeted. Anonymity itself is slowly being considered a crime. The word privacy will soon mean criminal intent."*[53] Roger himself was against the crackdown on such services and making them inaccessible even for legitimate users instead of fixing the underlying issues.

There were incidents of involvement and association of cryptocurrencies with illicit activities such as money laundering, fraud, and terrorist financing due to their pseudonymous nature and decentralized infrastructure. Banks were wary of facilitating cryptocurrency transactions to avoid inadvertently facilitating criminal activities.

The instances of cryptocurrency hacking and ransomware attacks further raised questions about the effectiveness of a decentralized and unregulated currency in monitoring the financial system. Ransomware attack cases began surfacing as early as 2013 when the CryptoLocker ransomware attack made headlines, locking out over 250,000 computers within a short span of four months.

It required the victims to pay in cryptocurrency or gift cards to reclaim access and unencrypt their hard drives or files. The resulting monetary loss from the attack was found to be around $3 million, and the following year, it was buzzed with the widespread news of CryptoWall, infecting various computer systems and demanding payment to gain access to a decryption program. Roger remembered that the damages accounted for multiple times higher than the attack the previous year, resulting in a loss of $18 million. The trend continued the following year, too, with TeslaCrypt initially targeting gamers and then expanding the scope of their attack. The ransom demanded to provide access to decryption keys ranged between $250-$1,000 in Bitcoin. Roger also recalled the Locky attack in 2016, which gained wide traction due to its high number of attacks on computer networks.

The highest number of attacks recorded by a source reported 50,000 attacks in one day. The virus would lock the files on the victim's computer, demanding a ransom payment in exchange for the decryption tool. The virus had multiple variants, but the central functions of all attacks remained the same. Although most of the attacks were reported in the US, Canada, and France were not spared from the attacks either. The ransomware attacks seemed inevitable and continued despite the efforts being made to curb them.

In 2017, users all around the world faced another setback when the news of 'WannaCry ransomware' made headlines. Crypto-ransomware either encrypts valuable files on computer systems or locks users out of their computers to demand ransom. It spread through computers operating Microsoft Windows and reportedly affected around 230,000 computers globally. During that time, Bitcoin and other cryptocurrencies became attractive tools for online crime and illegal activities. With each passing year, more names continued adding up, including Travelex, CWT, CNA Financial, Brenntag, Colonial Pipeline, and others.

In addition to such incidents, the cryptocurrency world also witnessed some of the biggest hacks, tainting the credibility of digital currencies and raising questions about privacy protection and security. The renowned hacking attacks on Mt. Gox in 2011 and 2014 were the first significant cases of crypto hacking that took users by storm. Roger anticipated that strict measures would be taken to prevent such attacks in the future. However, the reality proved otherwise. Four years after the second attack and the closure of Mt. Gox in 2014, the Japanese exchange Coincheck became a target of a hacking attack, losing around 523 million NEM coins. The coins were valued at $534 million at that time, and the president of the NEM Foundation described the attack as the most significant theft in the history of the world. Roger believed that the attack was even more significant than the Mt. Gox hacking, compelling new entrants to rethink their decisions to invest in cryptocurrency.

In 2021, a hacker's successful attempt to hack the 'Poly Network Defi platform' shook the world to its core by stealing around $600 million, including $33 million Tether. However, what shocked people even more was that after several attempts and requests from the platform, the hacker began cooperating in the return of the stolen funds. The hacker returned $300 million only after a couple of days, making everyone wonder if the hacker did it for a mere adventure.

In 2022, one of the most high-profile hacking attacks in the history of cryptocurrency happened when a 'Binance exchange, BSC Token Hub,' was hacked, causing a loss of around $576 million. The hackers created and withdrew 2 million additional Binance coins (BNB), causing the exchange severe loss. As cryptocurrencies continued gaining value, the magnitude of hacking attacks also kept increasing.

2022 registered another, and to date, the largest hacking attack of all time, when the Ronnin network was attacked. The hackers breached the network that supports the 'Axie Infinity' blockchain gaming platform, flying away with around $625 million worth of digital assets, including Ethereum and USDC stablecoins.

All these incidents and happenings added to the already existing challenges for cryptocurrencies to go mainstream as an alternative to the traditional banking system. However, despite the controversies and criticism from mainstream finance, the development of blockchain and its adoption beyond cryptocurrencies was never halted. Known as the *history of every "confirmed Bitcoin transaction,"[54]* the blockchain technology was officially launched in 2009, before the release of its first application, Bitcoin. The Bitcoin whitepaper outlined a decentralized digital currency system that relied on a distributed ledger to record transactions securely and transparently. Roger had been keeping an eye on it and considered the development of blockchain technology a significant milestone in the evolution of digital systems and decentralized networks. He had been witnessing the expansion of blockchain technology beyond its cryptocurrency origins to revolutionize various industries and sectors.

Intrigued by the transformative blockchain technology, Roger invested much time in understanding how it worked and what its benefits were. He discovered that blockchain technology works by creating a decentralized and distributed digital ledger that records transactions across multiple computers in a network. The process begins when a participant, let's say User A, initiates a transaction, such as transferring digital assets from one address to another. Besides the transfer of digital assets, executing a smart contract or recording data on the blockchain also initiates the process. Each transaction is cryptographically signed and contains relevant information, such as sender and receiver addresses, transaction amount, and timestamp.

Once created, the transaction is broadcast to the network of nodes (computers) participating in the blockchain network. These nodes validate the transaction's authenticity and integrity using consensus mechanisms, such as proof of work (PoW), proof of stake (PoS), or other consensus algorithms. Validated transactions are grouped into blocks that are cryptographically linked to the previous block, forming a chain of blocks (hence the name "blockchain"). Each block contains a unique cryptographic hash of the previous block, creating an immutable record of transaction history. Consensus mechanisms ensure agreement among network participants on the validity of transactions and the order in which they are recorded on the blockchain. Through consensus, nodes reach a shared understanding of the state of the ledger and prevent double-spending or fraud.

Roger considered the biggest benefit of blockchain technology to be decentralization. Instead of relying on a central authority to validate and record transactions, blockchain operates on a peer-to-peer network where every participant (node) has a copy of the entire ledger. The decentralization ensures transparency, security, and resilience against single points of failure or manipulation.

Another compelling benefit of blockchain technology is that when a new transaction occurs, it is broadcasted to the network and grouped with other transactions into a block. Miners or validators then compete to solve a complex mathematical puzzle to add the block to the blockchain. Once added, the transaction becomes irreversible and cryptographically linked to previous blocks, forming a chain of blocks. This enhances transparency across the blockchain.

Once recorded on the blockchain, transactions are tamper-resistant and cannot be altered or deleted without consensus from the majority of network participants.

This immutability ensures the integrity and trustworthiness of the data stored on the blockchain, making it suitable for applications requiring secure and auditable records. Roger regarded the development of blockchain as vital for the development of smart contracts. Blockchain platforms like 'Ethereum' support the execution of smart contracts, which are self-executing contracts with the terms of the agreement directly written into code. Smart contracts automatically enforce and execute the terms of the agreement when predefined conditions are met, eliminating the need for intermediaries and reducing the risk of fraud or manipulation. The transparency provided by blockchain technology enhances accountability, reduces disputes, and enables new applications such as supply chain traceability, provenance tracking, and digital identity management.

People believed that Bitcoin popularized blockchain technology, and Roger agreed to it to some extent, but he also believed that its potential applications extend far beyond digital currencies. He recognized that blockchain's decentralized and immutable ledger could be applied to various areas, and the time verified his anticipation as he witnessed the increasing use cases of blockchain technology. The emergence of alternative blockchain platforms and protocols designed to address specific industry needs has expanded the utilization of this transformative technology to various industries. From 2019 onwards, the crypto world has witnessed the wide adoption of blockchain technology in multiple sectors beyond cryptocurrencies.

In the healthcare industry, the incorporation of blockchain technology offered worthwhile benefits, including cost reduction, increased access to information, and streamlined operations. Roger came across healthcare platforms such as Chronicled, MEDICAL CHAIN, Nebula Genomics, and others that leveraged blockchain technology to streamline their operations and improve the functions for the users and consumers. Not only this, but the speculations about creating personalized treatment plans and medicines utilizing the transformative blockchain technology underscored its potential and impact. Other prominent areas where the applications of blockchain technology made a mark were money transfers and smart contracts. The years following 2019 witnessed a flood of cryptocurrency transfer apps saving time and money for its users.

With the utilization of real-time ledger systems, the elimination of third-party fees, and the eradication of bureaucratic rules and regulations, blockchain-backed money transfer systems disrupted the existing and traditional money transfer systems. Various companies in the US gradually adopted and incorporated blockchain technology within their operations to reap its benefits.

Over time, businesses identified that blockchain could improve supply chain transparency, traceability, and efficiency by providing a tamper-proof record of the journey of goods from their origin to the end consumer. It allows stakeholders to track and verify product provenance, authenticity, and conditions throughout the supply chain, reducing fraud, counterfeiting, and logistical errors. Large companies like Walmart and IBM began using blockchain to enhance their supply chain visibility and streamline processes.

Smart contracts, *"the programs stored on the blockchain that run when the predetermined conditions are met, eliminate the need for a middleman while enhancing the levels of accountability for the involved parties.*[55] This saved businesses significant time and money while providing them with peace of mind and ensuring compliance from all parties involved. These contracts revolutionized the business world, and their use cases ranged from private entities to public platforms. When Google introduced solutions for streamlining smart contracts, Roger's belief in its transformative power strengthened even more. He was glad to witness cryptocurrency and blockchain technology coming to the frontline and transforming people's lives.

Roger considered the development of 'decentralized finance' (DeFi) to be the most prominent and worthwhile application of blockchain technology. Ethereum's blockchain facilitated the development of decentralized finance (DeFi) applications that provide financial services without intermediaries. DeFi platforms like MakerDAO, Compound, and Uniswap offer decentralized lending, borrowing, trading, and asset management services, allowing users to access financial products and services directly from their crypto wallets. As Roger began counting, the list of applications of blockchain technology kept increasing, with use cases covering various sectors and industries.

Among the plethora of use cases of blockchain technology, one that Roger considered a significant step forward was the protection from fraud and hacking. Cybersecurity has faced several hacking threats, scams, and fraud attempts with the technological boom. The theft of essential personal information became a norm, affecting a significant portion of the population. Roger believed that utilizing a decentralized blockchain ledger to protect identity and personal information could be a significant difference in identity theft claims. He wished governments could adopt the technology for adequate data protection at the mass level, just like various companies incorporated blockchain-based databases and ledgers, allowing users to protect their information from identity theft risks.

Over time, the use cases of blockchain technology kept increasing and improving, opening ways for others to identify and utilize its potential. As Roger witnessed the development of cryptocurrency and its growing prospect for replacing the traditional banking system, he anticipated that besides simply investing in new cryptocurrencies, investors had begun analyzing the business plans for crypto start-ups, too.

Unlike earlier, when crypto was limited to exchanges, he was elated to see crypto projects in a vast range of industries, including gaming, sports, finance, and management. Although much work remained to be done to improve the system further and enhance its security, Roger believed that the crypto world was set off for exponential growth.

Chapter 5: The Role of Central Banks and Government

Roger once encountered a group of children fighting over something while on his daily stroll. As he took a turn near the street, he could hear the voices of kids coming from a dimly lit alley. Curious about what was going on, he entered the alley to check on the kids. As he approached them, their voices became clearer, and he understood that they were arguing about exchanging things with each other.

"Hey, Tommy, I'll trade you two shiny marbles for that rare baseball card," one boy with a red cap on his head exclaimed eagerly, showing off the shiny marbles in the palm of his hand. Tommy thought for a while about the offer and then said, "Make it three marbles, and you've got yourself a deal."

The first boy began pondering over it for a while and then said, "No, I can't give you three of them. If I did, I would only be left with two."

"Then I won't give you my rare baseball card. You can choose any other card from my collection," Tommy said, keeping the baseball card in his pocket.

"But I don't need other cards. I can offer two of my marbles in exchange for the baseball card that I want," the second kid stressed.

Roger couldn't help but smile as he saw the children negotiating. He had often seen these kids playing in the public park where he used to walk daily. It reminded him of his childhood when he and his friends would spend hours trading toys in the schoolyard.

"Looks like the barter system is alive and well," Roger remarked to a fellow bystander, who nodded in agreement.

"It sure is," the bystander replied with a chuckle. "Kids these days are always finding creative ways to get what they want."

As Roger continued to observe the scene, he saw the kids finally reaching an agreement after a while of discussion and negotiations. He decided to have a little conversation with the kids, anticipating to give them some worthwhile knowledge.

"Hi, kids. I just saw you exchanging marbles for some cards. Do you know people used to trade the same way in ancient times?" he asked them.

"Really?" the kids asked.

"Yes. If you want, I can tell you an interesting story," Roger offered, and the kids readily agreed. They slowly began walking towards the park, which was only a few steps away. After finding a nice place to sit, Roger started his origin story about money from its introduction to its current form.

"What were you saying about money?" One kid asked as he saw Roger lost in thought.

Without it, modern economies could not function. Roger thought about what he had read about money the other day. "Well, I assume you all have an idea about money," Roger began explaining to the kids.

"Money is something that holds its value over time, can be easily translated into prices, and is widely accepted."[56]

"But it wasn't always the same. The money you see now is not how it always used to be. Before taking its current shape, money underwent various stages of development. Before the introduction of currency, people traded using barter—*the direct exchange of goods and services without an intervening medium of exchange or money.*[57] However, the barter system wasn't that reliable. It had some flaws, and you have seen a glimpse of it in your exchange, too," Roger explained.

"The two major problems in the barter system were the lack of transferability and divisibility. For instance, if someone had a sheep or a cow to offer in exchange for goods and services they wanted, they were usually not able to successfully trade it for smaller or less-valued items; for instance, a sack of grains in exchange for a whole cow would be a ridiculous deal. Similarly, finding the person offering the thing you needed in exchange for the things you offered was a tiring task. If a person had meat to offer in exchange for rice, he not only had to find a person offering rice but also ensure that they would be willing to exchange the rice for meat. Seeing these issues forced the economies to think of a better system than bartering, and eventually, they decided on precious metals as their medium of exchange."

"Earlier, many different objects were used as money, including cowry shells, barley, peppercorns, gold, and silver. These things used to serve as a medium of exchange but had other downsides.

For instance, barley was a food item and took time to grow. In the case of its widescale consumption, the supply of money tends to fall. Similarly, other food items used in exchange for goods and services weren't reliable due to their perishable nature. The people didn't gladly accept items such as cowry shells due to their lack of value and usage. In such conditions, valuable metals such as gold and silver were believed to be the best medium of exchange. They served as a medium of exchange and had a durable store of value and a stable unit of account. In short, they solved all the problems that other commodities had. Besides other characteristics, they were easily transferrable and divisible."

Roger looked at the kids to see if they were still interested, and their keen attention to him proved that they were.

"Do you know when and where the first official currency minted was?"

"Not really. Doesn't every country have their own currency?"

"Yes, they do. However, the first time a currency was formed and issued was in China in 550 B.C. They created gold coins and used them as a currency. Government and authorized authorities minted standardized coins, providing a convenient medium of exchange with uniform size, weight, and purity. Governments began issuing paper money backed by gold reserves to meet the growing demand for currency and facilitate larger transactions. Later in the 19th century, the gold standard emerged as a monetary system."

"Gold coins had intrinsic value, meaning their value was derived from the original worth of the metals. Money became a universal language of trade. Instead of finding someone who wants what you have, you can use money to buy what you need from anyone, anywhere. It's like a magical key that unlocks endless possibilities. During the 17th and 18th centuries, governments began issuing paper currency backed by gold reserves to meet the growing demand for currency and facilitate larger transactions. *"Britain was the first country to adopt the gold standard system, which later became the international monetary system after 1870."*[58] Following suit after Britain, other countries of the world eventually adopted the same monetary system."

"What do you mean by the gold standard system?" a kid asked.

"A gold standard is a monetary system where a country's currency or paper money has a value directly linked to gold."[59]

Britain officially ceased the use of the gold standard system in 1931, while the US discontinued it in 1933. In most parts of the world, the gold standard system ceased in 1914 during World War I. After staying in the system for over 34 years, the Bretton Wood system replaced the gold standard system and, later, the fiat currency system.

The Bretton Woods system involved setting the gold standard to determine the exchange rate for various currencies. Following the Second World War, the victorious allies gathered at Bretton Woods in the United States. They signed an agreement to fix their currencies to the US dollar in an attempt to achieve financial stability and cater to the burning issue of inflation. The US government agreed to exchange $35 for an ounce of gold. The agreement remained influential until the 1960s, when it became apparent that the US did not hold sufficient gold to comply with the Bretton Woods Agreement requirements. Later, in 1971, US President Richard Nixon attempted to change the exchange rate to $38. That marked the end of its guarantee to exchange other currencies at a fixed rate.

As a result of this agreement, international trade continued using the US Dollar on this quasi-gold standard until 1971. By 1973, the rate was again changed to 42 US Dollars per ounce. From then on, the US Dollar and all other currencies were valued against other currencies alone. The international currency market then became a true fiat system without any vestige of a gold standard. Later, economic challenges like the Great Depression and the need for flexibility in monetary policy eventually led the governments to abandon the gold standard. The gold-backed monetary system was replaced by fiat currency systems that offered central banks and governments greater control over the money supply and interest rates. As he talked about the evolution of money, he reached into his pocket, feeling the familiar brush of paper currency against his fingertips. A subtle smile touched his face as he began speaking again, "Fiat money, they call it. The money you see nowadays is issued by the Federal Reserve and printed by the Treasury of the US Government, backed not by gold but by decree—a trust that the pieces of paper you hold can be exchanged for goods and services of equal value."

"Can you see what is written here?" he asked while showing the one-dollar bill to the group gathered around him. It now included kids and adults.

It says that *"Legal tender for all debts, public and private,"* showing that it can be used for the exchange of goods and services of equal value.

Unlike the limited quantities of precious metals that once anchored currency, fiat currency is boundless in terms of its supply. Its supply is as flexible as the policymakers find necessary. Similarly, the fiat currency is significantly different from the gold standard system. The gold standard and fiat currency systems represented two distinct monetary frameworks, each with its own characteristics and implications for the economy.

The gold standard provided a comparatively stable monetary environment, where the currency's value was tied to a fixed quantity of gold. It limited the risk of inflation and resulted in deflationary pressures during economic expansion. On the other hand, fiat currencies suffer from fluctuations in value depending on various factors. Although they offer higher flexibility, factors such as economic conditions, government policies, and even market perceptions can significantly affect their value. The second most prominent difference he spotted was that under the gold standard, monetary policy was restricted by the requirement to maintain gold reserves, which prevented policymakers from responding to economic downturns with expansionary measures.[60] On the other hand, fiat currency allows central banks to implement a wide range of monetary policy tools according to the economic condition and the need for economic growth and stability.

Roger believed that both systems have implications for financial stability. While the gold standard provided a reliable anchor for currencies, it could also exacerbate financial crises by limiting liquidity during downturns. Despite their downsides and the risk of inflation, fiat currencies offered more room for central banks and governments to ensure liquidity and stability in the financial markets during crises.

The story of the beginning of the banking system is as interesting as the story of the money. The history of the banks dates back to merchants and goldsmiths who used to lend money to individuals and also kept their deposits of money for safekeeping. This later turned into an organized business and continued until the formation of the first bank. As Roger began telling about the history of banking, he recalled how challenging it was to trace the details of the formation of the first bank. He found mixed views of people. Some regarded the Bank of Venice as the first true bank in the world, while others considered Banca Monte dei Paschi Bank of Siena (1472) to be the first bank in history.

The Bank of Venice is argued to have been established in 1157 in the flourishing trading hub of Venice, Italy. The Bank of Venice served several key functions that laid the groundwork for modern banking practices. It provided financial services, including advancing loans and keeping deposits for both the government and individuals. Another significant contribution of the Bank of Venice was the issuance of bills of exchange. These bills enabled merchants to conduct transactions without needing physical currency or precious metals. They allowed merchants to exchange the bills as evidence of a promise to pay a certain amount of money at a later date mentioned in the bill. The innovation greatly facilitated trade and contributed to the prosperity of Venice as a commercial powerhouse.

Roger believed that the Bank of Venice played a crucial role in the development of modern banking practices, including deposit-taking and loan advancement. Depositors could entrust their money to the bank for safekeeping, earning interest on their deposits over time. Meanwhile, borrowers could obtain loans from the bank to finance business ventures or investment opportunities. Earlier, the banks only performed the duties of keeping deposits and issuing loans. However, as time passed, the roles of the banks also evolved, leading to the creation of the central bank. The first central bank known in the history of the world was Riksens Ständers Bank (the Estates of the Realm Bank) in 1668. It all began in 1619 when Axel Oxenstierna proposed that there must be a bank in every town to cater to the issue of lack of coins and the sluggish circulation of money. The wars had already led to a shortage of precious metals such as gold and silver; therefore, people had already been actively looking for alternatives. In 1656, Stockholms Banco was founded as Sweden's first bank, and it issued the first banknotes in Europe in 1661. Despite the bank's failure, it still played a significant role in securing the value of money and ensuring its smooth circulation in the economy. Later, in 1668, the Sveriges Riksbank was founded from the remains of Stockholms Banco and appeared as the world's first central bank.

Being the country's central bank, the bank was responsible for issuing currency notes and regulating their circulation in the economy. Over time, other countries also established their own central banks. Britain led the way with the creation of the Bank of England in 1694, followed by the Bank of North America in 1781.

In the United States, the first bank was founded in 1781 when Congress chartered the Bank of North America as the first financial institution chartered by the United States and the first real bank in the country. At that time, it served as a de facto central bank, with the majority of shares held by the public. During that time, the United States was fighting the American Revolutionary War and needed funds to finance its defense activities. The Bank of North America raised money to support the ongoing war against Britain. The Philadelphia financier Robert Morris was appointed the bank's first superintendent. He had given a substantial amount of his personal wealth to support the war.

Later, in 1791, the first official central bank of the United States was formed when Congress chartered the First Bank of the United States for a 20-year term. Initially, the purpose of the bank was to lend funds to the government and businesses, control the supply of notes, and ensure the stability of currency. The formation of the first central bank was followed by the creation of 18 new commercial banks within a short span of five years. Before the formation of the central bank, there were only four commercial banks in the United States.

In 1910, after the panic of 1907—*the first worldwide financial crisis of the twentieth century*[61]—*a* group of banking executives had a secret meeting at Jekyll Island, which was a secluded island off the coast of Georgia. They believed that the existing banking system suffered from severe problems, posing a significant threat to the financial system. The participants expressed their concerns in a plan they wrote in their meeting and also in the reports of the National Monetary Commission. Later, a monetary reform movement spurred in the country, leading to the creation of the Federal Reserve System in 1913. The FED was formed as a result of the Federal Reserve Act of 1913, which was signed into law by President Woodrow Wilson. As a result of that legislation, the Federal Reserve System was established to provide a more elastic currency, adequate supervision of banking, and an efficient and equitable clearing system. Over the years, the FED became a symbol of financial power and intrigue, playing a critical role in our everyday lives and the monetary system.

As the discussion continued, some adults joined them while the kids began leaving one after another, and the story of the money ended.

"And what do you think about quantitative easing (QE)? The form of monetary policy in which a central bank, like the US Federal Reserve, purchases securities from the open market to reduce interest rates and increase the money supply,[62]" one of the persons sitting nearby asked.

"Yeah, the tool used by central banks to stimulate the economy when traditional monetary policy measures become ineffective. When the central bank purchases government securities or other financial assets from the market, new money is injected into the economy, increasing the money supply, lowering interest rates, and encouraging lending and investment. Central banks implement QE during times of economic downturn or recession to boost economic activity. By injecting liquidity into financial markets, QE aids in lowering borrowing costs for businesses and consumers while encouraging spending investments and lending. So, it creates a conducive environment for economic growth in a stagnant economy." Roger responded.

"QE can support government deficit spending by keeping borrowing costs low. In countries with high levels of public debt, it can help alleviate debt burdens by lowering interest payments on outstanding government debt. By driving down long-term interest rates, QE reduces the cost of servicing existing debt, making it more sustainable for governments to manage their debt obligations," another man added.

"That's right. However, I am a little skeptical about Quantitative Easing since it tends to create more inflation than conventional monetary policies.[63] Therefore, I believe that the central banks must be careful about the inflationary pressure when implementing this policy to prevent the risk of excessive inflation or asset price bubbles from forming," Roger said.

"Yeah, after all, QE is typically implemented as an emergency measure and is intended to be temporary. Central banks have strategies for unwinding QE once economic conditions improve and inflationary pressure emerges," the man replied.

"Yes. I believe that central banks and governments have a crucial role in ensuring the success of this policy. They must be able to communicate their policy intentions effectively and take care of factors such as the state of the economy and inflation dynamics." As Roger concluded his comment, everyone nodded in agreement.

"I've heard that cryptocurrency has the potential to modernize the banking system and resolve the underlying issues of the current monetary system," the man sitting beside Roger said.

"It all lies in its fixed supply, unlike fiat currency that can have infinite supply," Roger responded.

"Unlike cryptocurrency, the supply of fiat currency is controlled by the central bank of a particular country. *Fiat currencies are, therefore, subject to inflation, given that monetary authorities can print money at any time.[64] With policies like quantitative easing, central banks can increase the money supply whenever they need it, as they previously did during the US global financial crisis, the European sovereign debt crisis, and the COVID-19 outbreak. On the other hand, cryptocurrencies such as Bitcoin have a finite supply free from any centralized entity's control. Bitcoin has a fixed supply of 21,000,000 units and does not rely on the system of debts.[65]* The total number of bitcoins created in the system would never exceed this predetermined limit. This makes it less prone to the risk of inflation," Roger explained.

"But aren't cryptocurrency prices more volatile than fiat?" one of the standbys asked.

"*Yes, they indeed are. Bitcoins and other cryptocurrencies are more volatile than fiat in terms of value.[66]* Their demand and supply determine their value and prices; therefore, we see sudden hikes and falls," Roger answered. After a while, Roger left the park to walk back to his apartment and think about the discussion he had in the park. As Roger walked against the pavement in the pleasantly warm weather, the flicker of a new ticker on the street corner caught his eye: "China cracks down: all cryptocurrency transactions now illegal." Trying to absorb the gravity of the headline he had just seen, he stopped momentarily. Despite the news channel announcing it as a bold move showing the stringent approach of the country in an attempt to control and regulate cryptocurrency, Roger knew it was nothing more than a part of the global efforts of cryptocurrency regulation.

He recalled the time when, in 2017, Chinese investors were dominant players in the Bitcoin market, and the speculative market accounted for around 90% of the global Bitcoin trade; the country shut down local cryptocurrency exchanges. Two years later, the country officially banned cryptocurrency trading when the People's Bank of China stated they would be blocking access to all forms of cryptocurrency exchanges, domestic, foreign, and Initial Coin Offering websites. However, cryptocurrency transactions continued through foreign online exchanges. *"China, along with Saudi Arabia and Qatar, placed a complete ban on cryptocurrency trading in the country."*[67]

As he turned a corner, Roger found himself outside an internet café whose glass windows had posters raving about the virtues of blockchain technology and its potential to transform the world. As he stood there, reading the poster's contents, he looked at a group of people nestled around a monitor, concentrating on something displayed on the screen.

He assumed that they might be discussing the latest enforcement by the US Treasury Department, which had extended its oversight to include exchanges and wallets, casting a wide net over any entity operating within the crypto space. As he walked, he pondered Nigeria's stance and the regulations and measures taken by other countries. In Nigeria, the central bank prohibited local banks from servicing cryptocurrency exchanges, driving trade underground, away from the light of official scrutiny. South Korea's mandate for real-name accounts in cryptocurrency trading flashed in his mind.

"Adapt or resist," he whispered as he stepped out of the café and advanced his feet towards his apartment. He knew that the work being done in the cryptocurrency world was still incomplete as the government and the central banks took responsibility for regulating the cryptocurrency world. His phone vibrated with a message from a colleague: *"Russia proposed to recognize crypto as currency."*

"Another domino teetering on the edge of decision," he exclaimed, taking a seat in the cafe.

He then began reading an article on his phone about the governments around the world implementing regulations and restrictions on cryptocurrency in response to various concerns and risks associated with their use. The title of the article read "Regulatory framework set to expand." According to the article, the regulations aimed to address issues such as investor protection, financial stability, money laundering, and terrorist financing.

"Anti-money laundering protocols, know your customer requirements," he read aloud. Those were not just terms; they were the tightening screws of scrutiny. Various governments around the world were imposing AML and KYC requirements on cryptocurrency exchanges and other intermediaries to prevent money laundering, terrorist financing, and other illicit activities. The regulations required exchanges to verify the identity of their customers, monitor transactions for suspicious activity, and report any suspicious transactions to regulatory authorities. He knew that *"Anti-money laundering (AML) efforts consist of the laws, regulations, and procedures that are designed to prevent criminals from exchanging money obtained through illegal activities – or "dirty money" into legitimate income or "clean money."*[68]

As he read the article, he discovered that many governments require cryptocurrency exchanges and other service providers to obtain licenses or register with regulatory authorities. These regulations aim to ensure that these entities comply with AML and KYC requirements and adhere to basic standards of operation and security. Governments were also working on imposing taxes on cryptocurrency transactions, capital gains, and income generated from cryptocurrency-related activities.[69]

"So, the government wants the individuals and businesses involved in cryptocurrency transactions to comply with tax laws and contribute their fair share to government revenues. Let's see where it goes," he said while going through the remaining part of the article. It included more information about governments implementing regulations to protect consumers from fraud, scams, and other abuses in the cryptocurrency market. The regulations included measures to ensure transparency, disclosure of risks, and recourse mechanisms for investors whom fraudulent practices have harmed. *"After solidifying its position as the world's largest mining hub in 2018, China took strict action against the flourishing cryptocurrencies and banned the ICOs."*[70] *"Where some countries like China, Saudi Arabia, Egypt, and various African nations imposed a complete ban on the trading of cryptocurrencies, some other governments imposed partial ban or conditional restrictions on the use of cryptocurrencies for certain purposes, such as prohibiting or limiting their use for payments, investments, or fundraising."*[71] It also mentioned the regulations regarding governments monitoring cryptocurrency activities to detect and prevent illicit activities such as money laundering, terrorist financing, and tax evasion. They also considered the use of advanced technology and data analytics to track cryptocurrency transactions and identify suspicious patterns.

After reading the complete article, Roger deduced that overall, governments aimed to strike a balance between fostering innovation in the cryptocurrency industry and mitigating risks to investors, financial stability, and the financial system's integrity. Roger pocketed his device as his thoughts raced faster than his steps. Every country's stance towards cryptocurrency was crucial in determining not only the future of the digital currency but also the future of the financial systems of these countries. As he contemplated different aspects of the role of central banks and governments, the results of a survey began recalling in his mind that suggested that *"there could be 15 retail and nine wholesale CBDCs circulating among the public towards the end of this decade".[72]*

As Roger marched towards his apartment, he knew that the role of central banks and governments in maneuvering the complexities of monetary supply and inflation was more crucial than ever.

Chapter 6: The Volatility of Cryptocurrency

It was about time when Roger decided to get his hands dirty in the world of cryptocurrency by directly investing in it. He discussed his plan with one of his friends, who was a programmer and was already dealing with the cryptocurrency world.

"It's good that you want to dig deeper into the world of cryptocurrency," his friend said, "but beware of the dangers that lie ahead."

"What do you mean by that?" he asked.

"Well, you might have seen how rapid and unpredictable price fluctuations have been in the cryptocurrency world over short periods. Unlike traditional financial markets, where price movements are relatively stable, the cryptocurrency market dynamics are quite different. This market is known for its extreme volatility, and the prices of the digital assets here sometimes swing by double-digit percentages in a matter of hours or even minutes," he said.

"You're right. I've observed this with Bitcoin's price fluctuations. But how and why does it happen?" Roger asked.

"*Bitcoin's price fluctuations primarily stem from investors and traders hoping for an ever-increasing price in anticipation of riches.*[73] "However, as far as different cryptocurrencies are concerned, there are various factors that contribute to their volatility. The most popular among them include the forces of supply and demand, market sentiments, and some other factors," his friend began explaining. You know well that most cryptocurrencies, like Bitcoin, have a limited supply. This limited supply, combined with the increasing demand, drives cryptocurrency prices higher. For instance, Bitcoin has a fixed supply cap of 21 million coins. This makes it deflationary in nature, unlike fiat currency, which is inflationary in nature.

"So this means that as the demand for Bitcoin grows for any reason, its price tends to rise. Conversely, a decrease in demand or increased selling pressure can cause prices to fall," Roger said, and his friend nodded.

"But what about the cryptocurrencies such as Ethereum, which do not have a limited supply?" Roger asked.

"Although Ethereum has no maximum supply limit, it has a burn mechanism that checks the demands and supply of the cryptocurrency in the network, stabilizing its value. It is estimated that around $ 9 billion worth of Ethereum coins have been burned within 1.4 years.[74] As a result of the burning mechanism, around 2.8 million ETH tokens have been removed from the network, preventing the oversupply of ETH tokens in the network. Due to this, the ETH supply has been net deflationary.[75]

The token burning or token destroying involves sending tokens to an address from which they cannot be retrieved. This reduces the asset's circulating supply and leads to an ultimate contraction in the overall supply over time.[76] Even though the burning mechanism was initially implemented for Ethereum's gas fees regulation, it now plays a significant role in keeping the supply of Ethereum tokens under check."

"But supply and demand forces do not always affect the price of cryptocurrencies. Cryptocurrency prices are heavily influenced by market sentiment. Investor confidence, fear, uncertainty, and speculation all have an impact on the prices of cryptocurrency. Positive news or developments within the crypto space, such as regulatory approvals, technological advancements, or institutional adoption, can drive prices upward. Conversely, negative news, security breaches, regulatory crackdowns, or market manipulation can lead to sharp price declines."

"This makes sense since much of the trading activity in the cryptocurrency markets is driven by speculation rather than fundamental value. Since traders often buy and sell cryptocurrencies based on short-term price movements, it leads to exaggerated price swings."

"Yes. Some other factors also come into play. For instance, the regulatory environment can significantly impact cryptocurrency prices, including the regulatory announcements or actions by governments and regulatory bodies. Cryptocurrency markets are still young, and regulation uncertainty is a frequent visitor. You would have seen this when the news of impending regulations or bans on cryptocurrency activities in certain jurisdictions led to panic selling and price declines."

For instance, the news of bans, restrictions, and regulations in China and other countries such as Saudi Arabia and Qatar led investors to doubt the reliability of cryptocurrencies. Conversely, clear regulatory frameworks and favorable regulations can boost investors' confidence and drive prices higher. Moreover, compared to traditional financial markets, cryptocurrency markets lack liquidity. This means that large buy-sell orders can disproportionately impact prices. This lack of liquidity can exacerbate volatility, especially in smaller or less-traded cryptocurrencies.

"I think you forgot to mention the technological developments. Every software upgrade and protocol change within cryptocurrency networks tends to influence prices. Forks, upgrades, and other improvements to blockchain technology affect network scalability, security, and functionality, leading to changes in investor sentiments and ultimately affecting price movements."

"Crypto volatility seems to be something I haven't been paying enough attention to. I do have a higher risk tolerance, so I don't have to reconsider my investment decisions now," Roger said.

"No. See, this is how crypto volatility can take you for a ride. It's your job not to let it do so. My go-to advice to anyone investing in cryptocurrency is to diversify your investments. You know, diversifying an overall investment portfolio reduces the fluctuations of cryptocurrency on your net worth. Since it is a highly volatile asset, consider less as more when you invest in crypto if you're a new investor. *The rule of thumb (according to betterment.com) when investing in crypto is to invest less than*

5% of your total investible assets in cryptocurrency.[77] This lower percentage reduces your susceptibility and risk while offering you a decent share to leverage the value of cryptocurrency when it is high." However, for seasoned investors with longer time horizons, investing up to 10-20% in cryptocurrency can prove highly lucrative, provided they are willing to assume the risks associated with the high-risk, high-reward sector and possess a higher risk tolerance. Ultimately, the decision to invest in cryptocurrency must be evaluated on a case-by-case basis, taking into account the investor's unique circumstances and investment goals.

"Another excellent strategy is to use dollar cost averaging. *Dollar-cost averaging is the practice of investing a fixed dollar amount on a regular basis, regardless of the share price.*[78] This means that you buy a fixed and consistent amount of crypto each month, week, or day, regardless of the price. This is an effective strategy for developing disciplined investing habits when investing in different asset classes and securities. And lastly, something that most people tend to overlook is the significance of being intentional about monitoring your investment portfolio. Regular monitoring is important, but over-monitoring leads to stress and anxiety, especially if you stick to the screen during a down period. Refraining from constant performance checks during bearish market trends is crucial to avoid making a wrong decision under the influence of anxiety and panic." "To be fearful when others are greedy and to be greedy only when others are fearful." (Warren Buffett) Roger also researched and found that

Betterment.com offers an easy way to start a balanced crypto portfolio of 17 specialty selected cryptocurrencies, including BTC & ETH and other portfolios managed by the Gemini Trust Company (Cameron and Tyler Winklevoss) for a nominal fee of 1%.

The discussion with his friend encouraged Roger to search more about cryptocurrency frameworks implemented for triggering a deflationary trend in their values. Upon researching, he found Pepe, a memecoin launched on Ethereum, to be one of the top deflationary coins. *Deflationary coins are the cryptocurrencies, coins, and tokens that decrease in total supply every time a token transfer happens. A percentage of the transferred amount will be burned with every transfer.*[79] Pepe's no-tax policy, redistributive system rewarding long-term stakeholders, and the burning mechanism are a few factors appealing to the cryptocurrency community.

The cryptocurrency was created as a tribute to the Pepe the Frog internet meme created by Matt Furie, which gained massive popularity in the early 2000s.[80]

He also gained worthwhile insights about Baby Doge, a deflationary coin designed to become more scarce over time. He found it interesting that *all holders of Baby Doge will earn more Baby Doge, which is automatically sent to their wallet by simply holding Baby Doge coins in their wallet.*[81] He discovered that every transaction that happens on the Baby Doge network automatically leads holders to receive a 5% fee. In addition to these, he also found other meme coins, such as Pitbull, DogeBonk, Siba Inu, Dogecoin, and others, making headlines in the cryptocurrency world. Deeper research and analysis revealed that memecoin metrics were proving to be vanity metrics for desperate blockchains and failed to stimulate any true adoption. He considered the vanity metrics of memecoins and fake coins similar to the likes and comments on posts on social media that appear spectacular but have no substantial impact in real life. There are memecone millionaires and memecoin losers. Depending on your timing of entry and exit, it can be very lucrative.

Based on his research, Roger listed the tokenomics for the top five cryptocurrencies by market capitalization, along with a comparison of their price history and potential opportunities, to help determine which ones to invest in. For ease, he presented the whole comparison in a presentable tabular form to make the information accessible.

Crypto-currency	Tokenomics	Utility	Price History	Opportunity
Bitcoin (BTC)	-Fixed supply creates scarcity (21M) -Bitcoin mining every four years leads to a deflationary supply schedule	-Primarily functions as a store of value, similar to gold, but has comparatively limited smart contract functionality	-Has a well-established track record with significant price appreciation over the years	The limited supply and established status offer long-term value storage potential
Ethereum (ETH)	-Uncapped supply, but issuance is controlled through a burning mechanism	-ETH is used for transactions on the Ethereum network, powering various decentralized applications	-Ethereum's price has grown alongside the rise of DeFi and NFTs	Its utility and potential for future innovation in the dApp space offer exciting opportunities

Tether (USDT)	-Value pegged to the US dollar, aiming for minimal price fluctuations -Centralized issuance	-Tether tokens enable businesses, wallets, payment processors, ATMs, and financial services	-Price has remained relatively stable	-A popular choice for trading and hedging against crypto volatility
Solana (SOL)	-Inflatable supply with total supply capped at 1.5 billion SOL -Ongoing issuance of network rewards	-Used for transactions and fees on the Solana network, supporting a growing ecosystem of dApps	-Witnessed significant price growth due to its high performance and scalability potential	-The strong ecosystem and focus on DeFi can offer opportunities

Binance Coin (BNB)	-Quarterly burning of a portion of BNB tokens for gradual supply reduction	-Used for discounts on trading fees, participation in token sales on Binance Launchpad, and other functionalities	- Benefited from the growth of the Binance exchange and its diverse use cases	The token's utility and potential for continued ecosystem expansion present opportunities

Once Roger gathered all the information, he realized that the top cryptocurrencies offered diverse tokenomics with varying supply structures, utility functions, and potential opportunities. Along with established players like Bitcoin and Ethereum, newer projects such as Solana also offered unique growth potential within the broader cryptocurrency ecosystem. However, from his discussion with his friend, he understood that every investor, whether novice or experienced, should consider each cryptocurrency's tokenomics, technology, market cap, price history, and regulatory factors to assess investment opportunities as well as risk profiles.

During his research, the major price swings in the value of Bitcoin attracted Roger's most attention. The historic price swing of Bitcoin in 2017 hid various worthwhile lessons for everyone in the cryptocurrency ecosystem. He recalled late 2017, when Bitcoin experienced a historic bull run, reaching an all-time high price of almost $20,000 per BTC. At the beginning of 2017, Bitcoin's price hovered around $1000 until it broke $2000 in May.

The increasing trend continued until it reached $19,188 in December. It was a huge breakthrough for Bitcoin and the following cryptocurrencies, leading to increased public faith and confidence in them. This surge was fueled by growing mainstream awareness and adoption of cryptocurrencies and speculative buying from retail and institutional investors. People were both surprised and hopeful to see a further rise in the price. However, this price rally was followed by a significant market correction, with Bitcoin's price plummeting by over 50% in the subsequent months. Mainstream investors, economists, governments, and scientists began taking notice of the surge in Bitcoin's value. Other entities also realized the potential Bitcoin carried and began developing cryptocurrencies to compete with it. Following its peak in December 2017, Bitcoin's price entered a prolonged bear market characterized by a series of sharp price declines. By December 2018, Bitcoin's price had dropped to around $3,000, representing a substantial decrease from its previous highs. This crash was attributed to various factors, including regulatory uncertainties, security breaches at cryptocurrency exchanges, and concerns about the long-term viability of cryptocurrencies.

While Roger was still studying the major price swing in Bitcoin's value in 2017 and its underlying reasons, his phone beeped, indicating an upcoming notification. It was about news where the headline popped on his phone, "Bitcoin's surge to $73k put 99.76% of entities in profit, signaling the mature phase of a bull market.[82]

"What a coincidence! Is this another crash in the making after an extraordinary surge?" he thought while clicking on the news to explore complete details. It revealed that in the years following the 2017-2018 bear market, Bitcoin experienced a gradual recovery, with its price gradually climbing back towards its previous highs. By March 2024, Bitcoin's price had surpassed its previous all-time high, reaching a new peak of nearly $72,000 per BTC.[83] Firstly, Roger thought that it was another temporary price hike driven by unusual factors.

However, he later realized that the resurgence was driven by several factors, including increasing institutional adoption, growing interest from retail investors, and macroeconomic uncertainties that prompted investors to seek alternative stores of value.

Roger believed that it could be due to several factors, such as increased institutional adoption as more and more financial institutions are starting to invest in Bitcoin. Moreover, Bitcoin is a hedge against inflation, similar to gold, which could attract them during economic uncertainty. Additionally, innovations and advancements within the Bitcoin network or related technologies could also be fueling renewed interest.

Suddenly, Roger remembered the halving of Bitcoin, which was expected to happen in April 2024. He knew how significant this event was in the history of cryptocurrency to ensure its limited supply. He also knew that it had important implications for the supply dynamics and price of Bitcoin. Following a massive surge in Bitcoin's value, considering the historical record, he knew that halving always had a significant impact on the value of Bitcoin. So, he knew that the upcoming halving could raise the price of Bitcoin further, reaching a new ATH.

"Bitcoin halving is a periodic event that takes place after every 210,000[th] bitcoin block has been mined."[84]

Considering the fact that it takes around ten minutes for one Bitcoin block to be mined, 210,000 blocks are mined in around four years, and thus, Bitcoin halving takes place every four years. Since the last halving occurred in 2020, the next one is expected to happen in 2024, around the middle of April. The Bitcoin halving is a pre-programmed event built into the Bitcoin protocol that occurs automatically once the set limit of blocks has been mined. During the halving, the number of new Bitcoins created with each block mined was reduced by half, decreasing the rate at which new Bitcoins are introduced into circulation.

Since Bitcoin operates on a deflationary supply schedule, with a maximum cap of 21 million Bitcoins that can even be created, the halving event is crucial to gradually reduce the rate of new Bitcoin issuance, ultimately leading to a fixed and finite supply. When the halving occurs, miners' block reward for successfully mining a new block is cut in half.

This means that miners receive fewer Bitcoins as a reward for their computational efforts, reducing the rate of new Bitcoin creation. Since the halving creates a scarcity of available Bitcoins in circulation, it reduces the supply and, ultimately, leads to a bullish factor for Bitcoin's price, significantly increasing it. The halving event creates scarcity and can potentially increase demand relative to supply. This means that since miners currently receive 6.25 Bitcoin for each block mined, during the halving event in 2024, the reward will be cut in half, dropping to 3.125 Bitcoin per block.

A quick look at the price impact of the halving event revealed that every time, a price surge followed the halving event, even if it was temporary, and the new price would settle at a higher average than before. He discovered that during the 2012 halving, the price went from $13 to $1,152 in the following year. The same trend continued during the next halving event in 2016 when the price went from around $664 to $17,760 following the next couple of years. He also remembered the halving event that took place during the global pandemic, which still led to a staggering price increase from around $9,734 to $67,549.

However, the risk factors couldn't deny the potential cryptocurrency holds for investors. Robert remembered the surprising story of Glauber Contessoto, the "SlumDoge Millionaire" who went from rags to riches with crypto.

Coming from a humble family background, Glauber defined his lifestyle as really poor when his family moved to the US from Brazil. He came across cryptocurrency in 2021 when he heard about Dogecoin and decided to invest in it. With no disposable money in hand, he had to sell almost all of his stocks and borrow some funds to purchase Dogecoin. Fast forward to the tweets from Elon Musk a couple of months later that sent the price of Dogecoin shooting to the sky, rallying 37% within 24 hours.[85] The sudden surge made Glauber Contessoto a crypto millionaire. He found another investor, Mr. Smith's story, even more inspiring, who fulfilled his dream of touring the world with his crypto investment. Smith, a software engineer, worked at a large technology firm in Silicon Valley and made a good income. In 2010, when the price of Bitcoin was only 5 cents, he bought 20,000 Bitcoins for $3,000.

It was an experiment to test the potential of crypto growth, and Smith wanted to keep it for the long term to allow it enough opportunity to grow. Three years later, he saw the news of a 10% price rise in a single day and sold around 2000 coins. A few days later, the price hit $800, and he sold another 2000 coins. After earning $2.3 million with his trade and lots of Bitcoins still in hand, he quit his job and went on a trip around the world. An experimental investment led him to pursue his dream and live a luxurious life within a matter of days.

These success stories might have sounded too good to be true had Roger not witnessed them himself. One of his friends, Rachel, who was only a teacher, made her fortune in the crypto sphere with a meager initial investment. He still remembered when she lived from paycheck to paycheck in a rented apartment and knew nothing about cryptocurrency. However, after attending an after-party at a cryptocurrency conference, he decided to try her luck in crypto investment. She began putting her leftover paychecks of just $25 in cryptocurrency and dollar cost averaging. A few years into it, her holdings grew massively in value, reaching the seven-figure range and turning her life around. The price history revealed that the cryptocurrency market experienced a meteoric rise in market capitalization from billions to trillions of dollars over the past few years.[86] Before 2021, the total cryptocurrency market capitalization hovered in the billions of dollars for several years. While Bitcoin had seen significant growth, the overall market remained relatively small compared to traditional asset classes. The year 2021 witnessed a historic surge in the crypto market. Several factors fueled this growth, including the increased institutional adoption, retail investor interest, and the risk of DeFi and NFTs. By late 2021, the total cryptocurrency market capitalization reached a peak estimated to be in the range of $3-4 trillion dollars. Bitcoin itself surpassed a market capitalization of $1 trillion for the first time.

After observing the price fluctuations of Bitcoins over the years, the question that rose in Roger's mind was why Bitcoin had reached an all-time high (ATH) against some major currencies but not necessarily against the US Dollar (USD).

Some detailed research revealed that the US Dollar is currently considered a strong currency compared to some others. Several factors, such as rising interest rates in the US and global economic uncertainty, can increase demand for the USD.

This strength can make Bitcoin appear relatively weaker against the USD, even if its price in USD terms is still high. Moreover, if other major currencies, like the Euro (EUR) or Japanese Yen (JPY), are experiencing weakness due to specific economic factors in their respective countries, Bitcoin's value relative to those currencies could increase. This wouldn't necessarily reflect a rise in Bitcoin's value itself but rather a decrease in the value of the other currency. For instance, if Bitcoin is priced at $65,000 and the USD strengthens due to rising interest rates, it might take more coins of other currencies, such as Euros (EUR) or Yen (JPY), to buy the same amount of Bitcoin. This would make Bitcoin's price appear higher against those currencies. On the other hand, if other currencies weaken due to specific economic situations, it might take fewer Euros or Yen to buy the same amount of Bitcoin. This would make Bitcoin appear to have reached an ATH against those currencies.

Since Bitcoin's price is determined by supply and demand on cryptocurrency exchanges, trading activity can temporarily alter the price of Bitcoin in those currencies. For instance, the price you see might be quoted in a specific trading pair, like BTC/EUR or BTC/JPY.

One of the most worthwhile lessons Roger learned on his crypto investment journey was the significance of ensuring the safety of digital assets. After studying so much about cryptocurrency, he knew that, as an investor, you are responsible only for the security of your digital assets, and one of the ways to ensure their security is by choosing the right crypto wallet for them. As he dug deeper into the types of wallets for efficiently storing and managing cryptocurrencies, he came across custodial, self-custodial wallets, and cold storage devices, each with its own set of advantages and considerations.

"Custodial wallets are wallet services offered by a centralized business such as a cryptocurrency exchange.[87]"

He understood that in a custodial wallet arrangement, the service provider holds the private keys required to access and control the user's cryptocurrency holdings on their behalf. The individual user is not responsible for protecting the private key to the wallet. Rather, they rely on the service provider to safeguard their assets and perform transactions, making them convenient for beginners or those who prefer to delegate the responsibility of managing their cryptocurrency holdings.

Besides the apparent advantages of custodial wallets, he realized that they carried certain risks, including the potential for hacking, theft, or loss of funds if the service provider's security measures were compromised.

On the other hand, there are self-custodial wallets, also known as non-custodial wallets. They empower users with full control over their cryptocurrency holdings by allowing them to manage their private seed keys independently. Self-custodial wallets allow users to generate and store their private keys securely on their own devices, such as hardware wallets, desktop wallets, or mobile wallets. Therefore, users have the sole responsibility for safeguarding their private keys and ensuring the security of their wallets. This makes self-custodial wallets less susceptible to hacking or unauthorized access compared to custodial alternatives.

Among the various cryptocurrency wallets available for users, not all are self-custodial. Instead, some wallets, particularly those provided by centralized exchanges or online wallet services, operate on a custodial model where the service provider controls the private keys. To ensure maximum security, he realized that users must be careful when evaluating the features, security measures, and custody arrangements of any wallet solution they choose.

Initially, Roger considered custodial wallets to be the most viable; however, later on, he realized that they carried some inherent risks, too. The foremost risk associated with custodial wallets is their security vulnerabilities. Since the users entrust their private keys to third-party service providers, these wallets are susceptible to security breaches, hacking, and theft. Moreover, users face counterparty risk, where the custodial service provider may experience fraud, bankruptcy, or operational issues. This can lead to a potential loss or freezing of funds. Custodial services may require users to comply with regulatory requirements, such as identity verification and KYC (Know Your Customer) procedures. This carries the risk of compromising user privacy and anonymity.

On the other hand, some of the reasons he considered that justified the use of a self-custodial wallet were enhanced security, decentralization, privacy preservation, and resilience to third-party risks. Self-custodial wallets offer greater security and control over cryptocurrency holdings by allowing users to manage their private keys independently. Moreover, they align with the decentralized nature of cryptocurrencies, providing users with ownership and sovereignty over their assets without relying on intermediaries or centralized authorities. By eliminating reliance on third-party service providers, self-custodial wallets mitigate counterparty risk and insulate users from potential disruptions or failures of custodial platforms. These wallets catered to the risks associated with custodial wallets and, therefore, presented a more viable solution for the users. The user is then responsible for their security and seed key backups, as well as maintaining their crypto portfolio.

After exploring different types of cryptocurrency wallets, Roger reviewed his wallet's features, functionality, and custody arrangements. He looked for indicators such as private key ownership, the absence of third-party intermediaries, and adherence to principles of decentralization and user empowerment. He realized that he had been using a self-custodial wallet.

One day, while going through an online discussion, Roger saw someone ask about cryptocurrency wallets. Seeing the question, he couldn't stop his fingers from typing the answer. He knew how important it was to have the right information about cryptocurrency wallets before entering the cryptocurrency world. Refreshing his knowledge, he began typing,

"Cryptocurrency wallets can be of two types: hot and cold crypto wallets. The distinguishing characteristic between a hot and cold crypto wallet is that a hot crypto wallet is an online wallet that is always connected to the internet. In contrast, a cold crypto wallet is an entirely offline wallet that stores your crypto offline. Consider a cold wallet like a shield that enhances the security of your digital asset. Since the private seed keys are created and maintained offline, they are comparatively less prone to online hacking attempts. A hot crypto wallet is connected to the internet and can be accessed through software programs, whereas a cold crypto wallet is entirely offline and accessible through hardware devices."

"Can you give me some examples?" The user asked.

"Sure. Some of the most common examples of hot wallets include Coinbase Wallet, Exodus Wallet, MetaMask, Edge, Robinhood, and Trust Wallet. Whether hot or cold, a cryptocurrency wallet operates based on a combination of cryptographic principles and blockchain technology. When you create a cryptocurrency wallet, the software generates a pair of public and private cryptographic keys. The public key acts as your wallet address, which you can share with others to receive funds. The private key is like a password that grants you access to your funds, but it must be kept secret. The keys are stored digitally in a hot wallet on an internet-connected device, such as a computer or smartphone. Meanwhile, the keys are stored offline in a cold wallet, typically created on an offline physical hardware device and saved on an engraved piece of metal. You use your private key to sign a transaction to send or spend cryptocurrency from your wallet. This transaction includes the recipient's public key, the amount of cryptocurrency to be transferred, and any additional data required by the blockchain network."

"Which one would you suggest choosing among them?"

"I won't suggest anyone. When choosing a hot wallet, you must be mindful of various factors. For instance, wallet design, its fee, and available integration options. Similarly, cold wallets have their limitations and considerations. I would suggest you research all the available options before choosing the one that best fits your needs, but having a mix of hot & cold storage solutions for your portfolio is ideal," Roger said.

He recalled the pros and cons of hot wallets he experienced when he used one. Since hot wallets were internet-based, they allowed easy access for the users to perform several activities efficiently and from a range of devices. The best thing that Roger found out about hot wallets was that they were primarily free to use; however, he later discovered some wallets that required paying interest on the stored cryptocurrency.

Yet, hot wallets were not without their drawbacks. Initially, Roger came across some unencrypted hot wallets and realized that they were not as reliable as the encrypted ones. Not only were they vulnerable to hacks, but some hot wallets had legal restrictions and were accessible only in specified locations without using a VPN.

"At least cold wallets weren't as susceptible to hacking due to being entirely offline," he thought. The incidents of hacking and cyberattacks were the primary reason cold wallets gained rapid adoption and popularity. He remembered the USB stick-like hardware devices such as a ledger; that was how the cold wallets looked, costing around $50 to $200. Cold wallets are available in various types, including paper wallets, hardware wallets, deep cold storage techniques, and multi-signature wallets. The paper wallets are in the form of a document with public and private keys and a QR code printed on them to facilitate transactions. Hardware wallets are simply USB or smart devices. In contrast, deep cold storage enhances wallet security. It facilitates people who require minimal access to their wallets by storing hardware wallets in vaults or geo-separating parts of their seed keys to those wallets.

"Whether hot or cold, choosing the right type of wallet depends on factors such as security preferences, convenience, and the frequency of transactions. I prefer using a combination of hot and multiple cold/hardware wallets for my investment portfolio. According to my experience and suggestions from experts, the best security practice is to use custodial or hot software wallets for on- and off-ramping transactions to convert crypto into fiat and vice versa. Hot wallets are typically more convenient for frequent use and provide a quick mode for quick and easy transfer of funds.

Since regular transactions are in smaller amounts, the loss can still be bearable compared to the loss of large amounts of funds in your wallet. Once you have completed the transactions, you can safely use hardware wallets to store your crypto funds for the long term."

"And let me make one thing clear. Choosing the right crypto wallet is only the first step to effective crypto storage. Although cold wallets offer enhanced security features compared to hot wallets, they still require careful handling and safekeeping to prevent loss or damage. Properly securing and backing up private keys ensures access to digital assets stored in cold wallets. You can find countless dormant Bitcoin wallets whose owners either forgot or lost their private keys. So you must back up your crypto wallet's seed phrase—which is your secret recovery phrase. A seed phrase is a series of 12 to 24 random words that serve as your last resort to unlock your cryptocurrency wallet and its private keys.[88] This key is usually generated by your crypto wallet's software and derived from its private keys. Consider it the master password of your digital wallet. Upon its creation, it's imperative to record it accurately." he added.

"Never knew about that. Thanks, buddy," the user responded.

"But I think I need to emphasize more on the significance of ensuring the safety of your seed recovery phrase. Remember that losing your seed recovery phrase translates to losing all of your cryptocurrency funds stored in the wallet, and no one can help you recover them. And if someone else gets access to your seed phrase, they can use it to access your wallet and all the funds stored in it. Crypto is all about self-custody, so always have a backup," Roger wrote.

"Where do you suggest I should store my seed recovery phrase then?" the user asked.

"Well, keeping your seed phrase backup on paper is not viable as it can easily be lost or destroyed. You need to keep your backup in a way that is water, shock, hacker, and fire-proof. I recommend storing or engraving it on a metal card to ensure longevity. Then making sure to store it in a safe or a fireproof container," he wrote. "And do not share it with anyone, store it on any cloud-based service, or anything connected to the internet. Or else it would be susceptible to online security threats and hacking attacks," he added. A few other people also joined the conversation and began sharing their best practices for the storage of the seed recovery phrase. They also mentioned some names of popular metal seed key backup solutions, such as Billfodl, Cryptosteel, ColdTi, and Bitkee. Before exiting the discussion, Roger felt the need to mention that the best practice would be using a hardware wallet such as a ledger to transact and then revoke the approved contracts after the transaction is complete. Keeping private keys entirely offline when sending, receiving, or swapping crypto assets would be the best way to protect against online security threats and attacks.

While turning off his computer, Roger was thinking about the evolution of the cryptocurrency ecosystem. The cryptocurrency market continues to evolve, with ongoing technological advancements, regulatory discussions, and investor interest shaping its future. Since it is highly dynamic, it tends to fluctuate rapidly. Although market capitalization currently stands at trillions, the risk of volatility and the potential for growth and innovation persist.

Chapter 7: The Rise of Crypto-Assets and Investment Opportunities

"You don't know about NFTs? What are you even doing in the world, bro?"

Roger was sipping some hot coffee in his favorite café when he overheard a group of youngsters discussing NFTs. Their conversation naturally drew his attention as they were seated right beside him. As soon as one of them mentioned not knowing about NFTs, the other began booing out loud and mocking.

"Hey, calm down, everyone. Let me explain," one of the boys calmly said.

"I assume that at least you know that NFTs are non-fungible tokens. They are blockchain-verified assets that cannot be replicated or corrupted," he said.

"Unlike physical money and cryptocurrencies, they cannot be exchanged or traded for one another," he explained. "Every NFT is unique, and it can be anything, including a photo, video, audio files, art, collectibles, and other digital assets."

All sorts of people, celebrities included, jumped on the NFT bandwagon, enticed by their meteoric rise in fame and value. They were probably wishing to leverage the surging value of NFTs and make a fortune; however, not long after, their investments turned them into the biggest losers.

"Have you heard about Justin Beiber's $1.3 million investment in Bored Ape NFT? In just a year, its value dropped to $60,000."

"And he is not alone. Sina Estavi's story is even more tragic. He bought Jack Dorsey's first-ever tweet's tokenized version and called it the Mona Lisa of the digital world. Now, he is on the verge of losing it all since he couldn't find a reasonable bid. The last time I checked, it had reached its new all-time low, valuing $3.77."

"I heard the same about Madonna, Eminem, and Neymar Jr. too. They invested large amounts in the Bored Ape Yacht Collection and ended up losing all the money invested. The initial hype made everyone go bonkers for multiplying their investments, but now that the hype has slumped, investors are looking for a way to get rid of their NFTs and minimize the bleeding loss."

"Of course, what would you expect after an almost 90 percent slump in their investments?"

The conversation took Roger's mind a few years back when Quantum made headlines in 2014 as the world's first NFT. At that time, nobody knew that it could be sold for $1.47 million only seven years later. In 2015, Spell of Genesis became famous as the first blockchain trading card game. It was followed by Rare Pepes in 2016. These collectible cards facilitated the creation of the first crypto art market. Later on, in 2017, CryptoPunks came to the fore as one of the most popular early generative art projects that inspired the creation of ERC-721. One of the first NFT games built on Ethereum, CryptoKitties, was launched in the same year. It gained widespread media attention and massive traction from the people. It also facilitated the creation of Axie Infinity, an early Ethereum-based NFT game based on the "play-to-earn" model. The early breakthroughs set the stage for upcoming innovations such as Decentraland, NBA Top Shot, and Art Blocks in 2020 and Bored Ape Yacht Club in 2021. The famous Bored Ape Yacht Club is credited with starting the avatar craze and cementing NFTs as a pop culture phenomenon, something that compelled even celebrities to invest in NFTs and ultimately face massive losses.

"I feel like the meteoric rise of NFTs in 2021 was destined to end in a bloodbath that happened in 2022. Although BTC recovered after going down the drain, NFTs could never recover. Their prices kept going down. I don't think it will ever recover again." The boys' discussion brought his attention back to the present as he savored his leftover donut.

"You never know. Since it is volatile, it can go either way. It may recoup some of its losses in the near future. The boy said, Their discussion has now shifted towards other topics, while Roger thought that there was probably a flaw in the marketing of NFTs. Since they were only advertised as a must-have flex for the mega-rich, investors never realized their true potential."

Roger believed that you can never be certain of whether the value of NFTs has declined, regardless of the fluctuations and challenges experienced in the market. While the hype and speculative frenzy may have subsided, NFTs still offer unique opportunities for creators, collectors, and investors in the form of digital ownership, creative expression, collectability and scarcity, and innovation and experimentation. While the NFT market may have experienced periods of volatility and uncertainty, the underlying value proposition could still be compelling for the participants in the ecosystem.

In decentralized finance (DeFi), lending protocols are governed by predefined algorithms that facilitate automatic loans—allowing users to take on leverage.[89]

While searching for decentralized lending platforms, Roger came across Aave, an Ethereum-based protocol and a decentralized crypto lending platform offering automated crypto loans. However, it requires collateral in the form of cryptocurrency. Anyone wanting to borrow crypto must deposit one cryptocurrency and borrow others. The cryptocurrencies offered as a loan are only limited up to a certain percentage of the collateral value (loan-to-value). Since Aave utilizes smart contracts, the borrowing process and tasks such as loan term calculation, deposited collateral calculation, and cryptocurrency distribution are automated. The smart contracts facilitate the elimination of the third-party intermediary, leading to decentralized transactions. The lenders can also use this platform by depositing their funds and earning interest against them. The native token offered by Aave is called AAVE, which can earn interest through staking.

The impact of liquidation is still present in Aave transactions. If the value of the collateral deposited by the borrowers drops too far, the collateral may be liquidated. The operational framework of Aave was also interesting. Instead of directly matching lenders and borrowers, Aave allows lenders and borrowers to deposit their crypto funds into the liquidity pools, from which the assets are lent to qualified borrowers.

Automated Market Makers (AMM) maintain the liquidity of the DeFi ecosystem. They use liquidity pools, allowing users to deposit cryptocurrencies and facilitating liquidity. Unlike traditional buyer-and-seller markets, AMMs facilitate the automatic trading of digital assets without the need for permission. The framework behind this technology implies that the control should not be exclusive to anyone, and anyone must be allowed to participate. Decentralized exchanges (DEXs) have always faced liquidity issues. AMM addressed those challenges by allowing the liquidity of the liquidity pools to be determined by the number of assets in them.

The higher the number of pooled assets, the higher the liquidity and the easier the trading. However, the continuous liquidity provided by AMMs is not their only advantage. Besides making the trading of less popular currencies possible, AMMs also make trading accessible by allowing everyone to participate in trading by providing them with liquidity. The fees are also comparatively lower than those of traditional exchanges. Since they often operate without any centralized interference, they offer greater control and autonomy to the users.

Vitalik Buterin also emphasized the need for AMMs not to be the only available option for decentralized trading.[90] Instead, he highlighted the need for many other ways of trading tokens.

Eventually, three variations of automated market makers were launched, namely Uniswap, Curve, and Balancer. The most enduring model among them is Uniswap, which allows users to create a liquidity pool with any pair of ERC-20 tokens in a 50/50 ratio.

The decentralized crypto exchange (partially financed by Binance Labs) PancakeSwap is known for its low fees and fast transactions, where anyone with a crypto wallet can swap tokens or stake them in exchange for rewards.[91] Its high reward rates made it extremely popular in 2021; however, it also gained attention from scammers, who soon turned it into a haven for pump-and-dump schemes. Being an automated market maker platform, PancakeSwap has four key features: trading crypto tokens, earning rewards, winning prizes, and buying NFTs. PancakeSwap is more popular than other AMM platforms in the ecosystem because it was created on the BNB Smart Chain, which keeps fees low and facilitates quicker transaction processing. Binance Smart Chain (BSC) is a blockchain network developed by Binance, one of the largest cryptocurrency exchanges in the world. Launched in September 2020, BSC is designed to provide a high-performance, low-cost platform for creating decentralized applications (DApps) and executing smart contracts. It operates as a parallel chain to Binance Chain, offering compatibility with the Ethereum Virtual Machine (EVM) and supporting the Ethereum ecosystem's tooling, including wallets, explorers, and developer tools. BSC features a consensus mechanism known as Proof of Staked Authority (PoSA), which combines elements of

Proof of Stake (PoS) and Byzantine Fault Tolerance (BFT) consensus algorithms. This consensus mechanism enables fast transaction finality and high throughput, with block times of approximately three seconds and transaction fees significantly lower than those on the Ethereum network.[92]

Other popular AMMs, Uniswap and SushiSwap, are built on Ethereum, which charges higher gas fees and offers lower transaction speeds due to congested networks. SushiSwap is a decentralized exchange (DEX) protocol and automated market maker (AMM) built on the Ethereum blockchain. However, it has expanded its operations to other blockchain networks, including Polygon. As one of the leading DEX platforms, SushiSwap enables users to trade a wide range of tokens, provide liquidity to liquidity pools, and earn rewards through yield farming. By integrating with Polygon, SushiSwap leverages the network's scalability and low transaction fees to offer users a more efficient and affordable trading experience.

Only a few months after its creation, BSC became one of the largest decentralized crypto exchanges in terms of the amount deposited by its users. As Ethereum's high gas fees raised scalability challenges for the blockchain, a solution was formulated in the form of Polygon.[93] The stack of protocols, Polygon, was aimed at fixing Ethereum's scalability issues and became the driving force behind transformative developments in the crypto space. Polygon, formerly known as Matic Network, is a layer two scaling solution for Ethereum that aims to improve scalability, reduce transaction costs, and enhance the user experience on the Ethereum blockchain.[94] It achieves this by utilizing sidechains, also known as "commit chains," which are interoperable with the Ethereum mainnet. Polygon provides developers with a framework to deploy scalable and customizable blockchain networks, enabling the creation of decentralized applications (DApps) with high throughput and low latency.

Over time, Polygon has become the driving force behind transformative developments in the crypto space. Preon is a decentralized lending protocol that allows users to borrow against their crypto as collateral and seize new opportunities all at 0% interest. Loans are paid out in $STAR (a USD-pegged stablecoin) with a minimum maintained collateral ratio of 110%. Preon exclusively accepts yield-bearing tokens as collateral, allowing borrowers to leverage-farm their position. This makes Preon one of the few lending protocols that charges no interest for leverage-farming. $STAR can be redeemed for $1 of underlying collateral, minus protocol fees. By leveraging Polygon's scalability and low transaction fees, Preon Finance aims to provide users with a seamless and cost-effective lending and leveraging experience. Benefits include liquidity without selling, flexible loan terms, instant loan approval, and repeatable borrowing. It is a zero-interest lending protocol that offers unique lending opportunities. More info can be found at (preon.finance).

Beefy Finance is a decentralized yield optimizer platform that operates on various blockchain networks, including Polygon. It automates the process of maximizing yield farming returns by optimizing the compounding of assets across different DeFi protocols. Users can deposit their assets into Beefy Finance's vaults, and the platform's algorithms automatically allocate these assets to the most lucrative yield farming opportunities available on the Polygon network. Using Beefy Finance, users can earn rewards passively without actively managing their DeFi investments.

The top projects in the Polygon ecosystem are necessary to keep an eye on as they exemplify the potential for decentralized finance and blockchain to change the way we interact with the physical world.

The top projects among them include Aave, Gamma, QuickSwap, and Superfluid. Aave stands out as a cornerstone of the DeFi space, offering decentralized lending and borrowing services on various blockchains, including Polygon and Ethereum. It has a high rank in Total Value Locked (TVL) due to its liquidity mining incentives and simple interface. Gamma, on the other hand, is a yield optimization marvel, providing automated and concentrated liquidity management. QuickSwap is renowned for offering speedy trades at competitive prices, ranking it as a top DeFi protocol on Polygon. Superfluid has revolutionized payments on the blockchain, allowing users to streamline rewards management. It has proven to be an essential tool for the integration of cryptocurrencies into daily life. Besides these options, Tangible stands out for its unique features. It is an ecosystem for tokenized real-world assets that utilize real USD, a native yield stablecoin backed by real estate.[95] The platform allows users to purchase valuable physical goods using real USD. The transaction results in the minting of a tangible non-fungible token (TNFT), which can be transferred, sold, or redeemed for the item purchased.

GameFi, short for "Game Finance," refers to the intersection of blockchain technology, decentralized finance (DeFi), and game theory.[96] It combines elements of gaming, such as non-fungible tokens (NFTs), virtual assets, and play-to-earn mechanics, with financial services like staking, lending, and yield farming. It aims to enhance users' interest in a particular blockchain project, deepening users' relationships with a specific cryptocurrency. The platform offers players the opportunity to participate in various gaming activities to earn rewards. The rewards can include tokens, NFTs, or other digital collectibles. They can then be utilized within the game or traded on decentralized exchanges (DEXs) for other cryptocurrencies.

As Roger delved deeper into GameFi platforms, he learned that these platforms often feature decentralized games, where ownership and control of in-game assets are recorded on the blockchain. This framework ensures transparency, security, and interoperability. Players can buy, sell, and trade these assets freely, creating a vibrant ecosystem of virtual economies. Moreover, GameFi projects may incorporate DeFi protocols to offer additional financial services to players, such as liquidity mining, yield farming, and token staking. This allows players to earn passive income while engaging in gaming activities.

GameFi represents an innovative fusion of gaming and decentralized finance, offering new opportunities for players to monetize their gaming experiences and participate in emerging digital economies. Thinking of leveraging the potential of GameFi, Roger discovered some popular games such as Axie Infinity and Decentraland. Both games were based on the P2E model, with collectibles and NFTs as rewards. He also found other games, including The Sandbox, Cryptokitties, Gods Unchained, and Splinterlands. The types of games varied; however, they all utilized P2E models and allowed players or users to monetize their gaming experience. He consulted some experts to gain advice on how to access GameFi platforms. They advised him to begin with a small investment of time and resources into these platforms to test their features and withdrawal policies. This will allow new gamers like him to gauge the platform's reliability without risking a significant loss.

To have first-hand experience, Roger selected a platform and checked the requirements. It required him to create an account after sharing some basic personal information and setting up a wallet address to receive and store rewards. Once he played the game and collected some rewards, he checked his balance in his wallet. Although the rewards were transferred to his wallet, he still could not retrieve them as the minimum withdrawal limit had not yet been reached. Once the minimum limit was reached, the platform did not ask for any additional withdrawal fees for the conversion of the earned rewards. However, he discovered some other platforms that required fees for converting earned tokens into fiat currency or other digital assets.

He also got the opportunity to discuss Metaverse, the technology that is envisioned to provide users with a real-like experience in a video-game-like world. Unlike Mark Zuckerberg's claim that Metaverse would be the future of the internet, the technology turned out to be a fad that couldn't pass the test of time and died not long after its introduction. Despite the hype surrounding the platform's introduction, the Metaverse could not lead a healthy life, and it later turned out that the business ideas and market projections it offered were based on vague promises. Despite the initial hype, people were reluctant to use it when given a chance. It showed that Meta could not convince people to use the product on which the company has staked its future. As the hype around generative Artificial Intelligence grew, Metavese's charm began fading and eventually vanished completely. Considering people's lack of trust and interest in the technology, the companies that had earlier adopted the idea also stepped back. From Walmart ending its Roblox-based Metaverse projects to Disney shuttering its Metaverse division, Meta's promise of Metaverse being the future also ended.[97]

***

One day, while searching for the latest trends in the cryptocurrency ecosystem, Roger saw several headlines about meme coins. Meme coins have also gained his attention due to their unique nature and popularity. He knew they had played a significant role in the widespread popularity of cryptocurrency.

Upon researching more about them, he discovered that meme coins, such as Pepe and Shiba Inu (SHIB), have gained significant attention in cryptocurrency due to their viral nature and community-driven marketing. These coins typically originate from internet memes or popular culture references and often lack fundamental utility or intrinsic value. PepeCoin, for example, is named after the internet-famous character Pepe the Frog and initially gained popularity as a meme within specific online communities. Similarly, the Shiba Inu coin, inspired by the Dogecoin meme, features the image of the Shiba Inu dog breed and has garnered a dedicated following.

Roger knew that before investing, he must first check out the trends and see the extent to which the investors realized their potential. His research revealed that while meme coins may attract investors seeking quick profits or participating in meme culture, they are often associated with high volatility and speculative trading. Many meme coins lack real-world use cases or underlying technology, leading to concerns about their long-term sustainability and potential for manipulation.

He also realized that investing in meme coins carries significant risks, as their value can fluctuate dramatically based on social media trends, celebrity endorsements, and market speculation. Since decentralized finance is unregulated, DeFi protocols are well known for scammers to make fast money. Additionally, regulatory scrutiny and security vulnerabilities pose additional challenges for meme coin projects. Despite these risks, meme coins continue to attract attention and investment, fueled by social media hype and speculative trading activity. However, investors should exercise caution and conduct thorough research before participating in meme coin markets.

One common way scammers may utilize this method is through pump-and-dump schemes. Pump-and-dump schemes involving new coins are a common occurrence in the cryptocurrency space. In these schemes, a group of investors artificially inflates the price of a newly launched or low-volume cryptocurrency by coordinating buying activity, often through social media platforms or chat groups. Once the price reaches a certain level, the orchestrators sell off their holdings, causing the price to plummet and leaving other investors with significant losses. These schemes exploit market manipulation tactics and prey on inexperienced investors, who may fall victim to the hype surrounding a new coin.

One thing that Roger noticed during his exploration journey was the widespread popularity of Telegram and Discord channels. Telegram and Discord channels are popular communication platforms cryptocurrency enthusiasts and communities use to discuss market trends, share investment strategies, and participate in initial coin offerings (ICOs) or token sales. These channels can serve as valuable sources of information and networking opportunities for investors seeking insights and opportunities in the crypto space. However, they can also be hubs for misinformation, pump-and-dump schemes, and fraudulent activities, highlighting the importance of conducting thorough research and exercising caution when engaging with such communities.

Roger was lucky to know these schemes beforehand rather than learning them the hard way. One of his friends told him about scams involving contract locks and liquidity manipulation that are prevalent in the cryptocurrency market, particularly in decentralized finance (DeFi) and token projects. In these scams, developers may promise high returns or innovative features to attract investors, only to disappear with investors' funds or manipulate liquidity pools to inflate token prices artificially. Contract locks, which restrict access to smart contract functions or funds, can be used to create a false sense of security among investors. At the same time, insufficient liquidity can make it challenging for investors to sell their tokens at fair market prices.

The biggest crypto scam schemes in DeFi included the rug pull and honeypot. The rug pull is the same as its name implies. Investors or developers with significant token supply holdings play a significant role in promoting the coin and creating hype. They might artificially increase your investment's value and then cause it to decline massively. The only way to minimize the danger of becoming rug-pulled is to consider the liquidity, the proportion of the top holders, and the existence of the minting function.

An even more dangerous scheme is a honeypot, where scammers fool investors into investing some funds in a seemingly great token and locking their ETH or BNB using a smart contract. To protect oneself from this scam, one must first analyze or find an independent audit of the smart contract code to ensure fair play and then simulate the transaction on a test chain.

"Smart contracts are self-executing agreements that are stored on a blockchain. They are used to automate various processes and transactions and are used in many blockchain applications, such as decentralized finance (DeFi), non-fungible tokens (NFTs), and more."[98]

Examining a token's smart contract audit is an effective way to mitigate a honeypot and other risks. A smart contract audit involves a detailed analysis of the contract's code to determine its authenticity. The more Roger learned about different scamming techniques, the more he realized the significance of due diligence, skepticism, and risk management when investing in cryptocurrency projects.

The start of 2024 witnessed a watershed moment for cryptocurrency investment with the SEC's long-awaited approval of several spot Bitcoin ETFs.[99] As the experts have already predicted, the decision opened the door for mainstream investors to gain exposure to Bitcoin through a familiar avenue: tradable funds on brokerage accounts. This move simplified crypto investing and potentially made it safer by eliminating the need to interact with cryptocurrency exchanges, which can be prone to security risks. Roger knew that Bitcoin ETFs could be a game changer in cryptocurrency. His expectations turned out to be true when the rollout of Bitcoin ETFs turned out to be a resounding success. Trading volumes soared, reflecting a surge in investor interest. These ETFs offer significant advantages over directly buying Bitcoin on an exchange, including added convenience, enhanced security, and accessibility.

Roger discovered that, with the Bitcoin ETF hurdle cleared, investor focus has shifted towards Ethereum ETFs. Ethereum, the second-largest cryptocurrency, underpins a popular blockchain platform for decentralized applications (dApps). Several applications for Ethereum ETFs are currently under review by the SEC. While approval is widely expected, it might not be a smooth ride.[100] The SEC might take a more cautious approach due to underlying differences in how Ethereum's network operates compared to Bitcoin's. However, experts anticipate that a legal challenge similar to what paved the way for Bitcoin ETFs could ultimately lead to broader SEC approval for Ethereum ETFs, which could be an easy way to diversify your investments into crypto assets.

***

Like any other beginner, Roger initially considered the stock market the only investment option available. However, as he delved deeper, he realized that when it comes to investment opportunities in various digital and real assets, the possibilities are pretty diverse and extend beyond traditional stock markets. They include real estate investments, precious metals such as gold and silver, promissory notes and private lending, cryptocurrencies, and even artwork. Each investment opportunity involves different investment strategies that investors usually employ to maximize their profits. Real estate investments are considered one of the least risky due to their stable value and utility. Similarly, people prefer buying precious metals such as gold, silver, and platinum since they can be stored for an extended period and are a good store of value. The investment in artwork was something new for him.

After a lot of trial and error, Roger realized that investing in art could be a long-term and reliable investment because it is capable of holding its value over time.[101] The return on an art investment is often considered similar to a fixed income that might rival bonds. Unlike stocks or other investments, art does not tend to go up and down in value based on market fluctuations. Evidence of this movement was seen during the 2020 pandemic, during the economic downturn. During that time, the slow economic activity led to significant fluctuations in other markets, whereas the art market maintained its stability. One key reason for this value trend is that the value of investment-grade art is independent of most external events and, therefore, has the tendency to increase steadily as the years go by. However, he also discovered the other side of the picture, revealing that although art is a reliable investment, it lies in the long-term asset class. This means that it is a non-liquid asset and cannot be quickly exchanged for cash. Liquidating art involves a lengthy process of art appraisal, conducting an auction, and finding the appropriate buyer. Therefore, Roger considered it appropriate to diversify his portfolio and not his primary investment. However, he was primarily interested in discovering the potential of cryptocurrency investments.

The market forecasts and projections offered encouraging insights. He discovered that the global cryptocurrency market is projected to grow from $910.3 million in 2021 to $1,902.5 million in 2028 at a CAGR of 11.1% in the forecast period 2021-2028.[102] He also learned that experts considered cryptocurrencies different from the Tulip Craze. The meteoric rise of Bitcoin and other cryptocurrencies has drawn comparisons to the infamous tulip mania of the 17th century. However, unlike tulips, cryptocurrencies are backed by something more substantial: a powerful combination of cryptography, code, and real-world utility. He had heard about the tulip craze of the 1630s, which was a period of extraordinary speculation in the Netherlands. Tulip bulb prices skyrocketed, fueled by a combination of factors, including the rarity of the tulips, the social status attached to them, and the speculative mania that ultimately led to a dramatic crash.

In the tulip craze, the value of the bulb was purely based on perception and social trends. There was no underlying utility or real-world use case. This stands in stark contrast to cryptocurrencies. Cryptocurrencies are digital assets secured by cryptography. They operate on decentralized networks powered by code, eliminating the need for a central authority like a bank. This empowers users with greater control over their finances. What differentiates cryptocurrencies from tulips is their utility, underlying technology, and limited supply. Cryptocurrencies can be used for various purposes, including making payments, storing value, and accessing decentralized applications (dApps). They leverage blockchain technology, a secure and transparent digital ledger system that underpins trust and immutability. Many cryptocurrencies, like Bitcoin, have a capped supply, preventing inflation and potentially contributing to long-term value.

Once Roger learned about various investment opportunities, he looked for different ways to invest in cryptocurrency and other digital assets. His research yielded worthwhile results, and he shortlisted some of the investment strategies. One of them was day trading. Day trading involves buying and selling financial assets within the same trading day, aiming to profit from short-term price fluctuations. Day traders execute multiple trades throughout the trading day, aiming to capitalize on small price movements.[103] They often employ technical analysis techniques, such as chart patterns, indicators, and volume analysis, to identify short-term trading opportunities and make rapid buying and selling decisions.

One common strategy employed by day traders is the use of initial and ride-up stop loss orders to manage risk and protect against potential losses. When initiating a trade, day traders typically set an initial stop loss order at a predetermined price level below the entry point. This serves as a safety net to limit potential losses in case the trade moves against them. The initial stop loss level is determined based on factors such as the trader's risk tolerance, the volatility of the asset being traded, and technical analysis indicators.

On the other hand, there is ride-up stop loss. As the trade moves in the trader's favor and the price of the asset increases, some day traders employ a ride-up stop loss strategy to protect their profits. With this approach, traders adjust their stop loss orders upward, trailing behind the rising price of the asset. This allows them to lock in gains and protect against potential reversals or market fluctuations. The ride-up stop loss level is typically set at a predetermined percentage or dollar amount below the current market price, ensuring that profits are preserved while still allowing room for the asset to continue to appreciate. Day trading requires discipline, risk management, and a thorough understanding of market dynamics. Traders must be vigilant and responsive to market conditions, as trades are executed quickly, and positions are typically held for only a short period.

Roger figured out other ways for individual investors to invest in cryptocurrency, including buying and holding (HODLing Hold On for Dear Life), which is the most common and straightforward investment strategy. This strategy is where investors purchase cryptocurrencies intending to hold them for an extended period, typically years, in anticipation of long-term price appreciation.[104] Investors believe in the potential of the cryptocurrency they are buying and hold onto it through market fluctuations, aiming to capitalize on significant price increases over time.

Investors can also opt for trading cryptocurrency. Trading involves buying and selling cryptocurrencies over short timeframes, ranging from minutes to days, to profit from price volatility. Day traders execute multiple trades within a single day, while swing traders hold positions for several days or weeks. Traders use technical analysis, chart patterns, indicators, and market trends to make informed trading decisions and attempt to generate profits from short-term price movements. Another popular method is mining, which is akin to digging for digital gold.[105] Mining involves validating and processing transactions on a blockchain network using specialized computer hardware and software. Miners are rewarded with newly minted cryptocurrency tokens as well as transaction fees for their efforts in maintaining the network's security and integrity. While mining was once profitable for individual miners using consumer-grade hardware, it has become increasingly competitive and resource-intensive. Significant investments in specialized mining equipment like ASICs and access to cheap electricity are recommended for more profitability.

Finally, investors can also invest using staking, which involves actively participating in the operation of a proof-of-stake (PoS) blockchain network by locking up a certain amount of cryptocurrency as collateral to validate transactions and secure the network. It involves locking digital tokens to a blockchain network to earn rewards—usually a percentage of the tokens staked.[106] Participants receive staking rewards in return for staking their coins, typically in the form of additional cryptocurrency tokens. Staking provides investors with an alternative way to earn passive income from their cryptocurrency holdings while contributing to the security and decentralization of blockchain networks.

After learning about various investment opportunities in the cryptocurrency ecosystem and beyond, Roger realized that there were some key considerations to always adhere to to ensure investments' safety and viability. The first one is that volatility is key. Both Bitcoin and Ethereum are known for their price fluctuations. This inherent volatility translates to risk, and ETFs do not eliminate that risk. The second most important thing for any investor is to do their own research. Just like with any investment, thorough research is crucial before diving into any investment opportunity in the cryptocurrency world and beyond. One must understand the underlying asset, the specific investment structure, and any associated fees. Lastly, one must invest wisely. Cryptocurrency ETFs and other investments are a new frontier, and investors should carefully assess their risk tolerance and overall investment goals before allocating any portion of their portfolio to them.

Chapter 8: Blockchain Mining and its Impact on the Environment

Ever since Roger explored the investment opportunities in the cryptocurrency industry, he has been intrigued by the idea of mining. He knew that mining involves solving complex mathematical algorithms or puzzles to validate and add transactions to the blockchain. *This process is crucial for the security and smooth functioning of blockchain networks. It is essentially a cryptographic competition to add blocks or records to cryptocurrency's ever-expanding blockchain network.*[107] Despite the significance of this process, its impact and the associated environmental risks make it a controversial phenomenon. It all links back to the mechanism for reaching a globally decentralized consensus on a valid blockchain called the proof-of-work algorithm.[108] It is a consensus algorithm that governs the process of transaction approval and verification on the blockchain network. The cryptographic hash function used in Bitcoin mining is SHA-256, which stands for Secure Hash Algorithm 256-bit. *"It is an unkeyed cryptographic hashing function that takes an input of variable length and produces a 256-bit long hash output."*[109] It takes an input and produces a fixed-size string of bytes, making it nearly impossible to reverse-engineer the original data. In the Bitcoin network, miners compete to verify and add new transactions to the blockchain. To do this, they must solve a complex mathematical puzzle using

SHA-256. This puzzle is referred to as the Proof-of-Work (PoW) algorithm.

When miners confirm blocks with transactions, they receive rewards for their respective work. Every mining pool has a different mining power that affects the probability of finding blocks with transactions. These chances are proportional to each mining pool's hashing power.[110]

"Hashing is the process of generating a value from a text or a list of numbers using a mathematical function known as a hash function. A hash function is a function that converts a given numeric or alphanumeric key to a small practical integer value. The mapped integer value is used as an index in the hash table."[111]

Since its inception in 2009, the Bitcoin network has undergone various revisions by various programmers. This increased the number and power needed for machines running the proof-of-work algorithm (mining), which provides security and resilience for Bitcoin. As a result, their combined computational power also increased exponentially, exceeding the combined number of computing operations of the world's top supercomputers. Miners use specialized hardware and software to perform these computations and, in return, are rewarded with cryptocurrency tokens such as Bitcoin, Litecoin, and others. Bitcoin's self-regulated mechanism, difficulty adjustment, also plays a significant part in ensuring the security of the network. The hardcoded time of block generation on the Bitcoin blockchain is ten minutes per block. This speed is crucial to keep the inflationary rate under check and ensure that the amount of Bitcoins mined and circulated remains under control. If this speed is decreased for some reason, it might lead to higher-than-usual mining, increasing the number of bitcoins in circulation. The difficulty adjustment phenomenon maintains this mining speed, ensuring the deflationary nature of Bitcoin persists, adjusting every two weeks.

As Bitcoin evolved over the years, so did the blockchain network and computer mining hardware. As a result, mining methods also evolved. The cryptocurrency ecosystem witnessed the transition from CPU (Central Processing Unit) to GPU (Graphic Processing Unit) mining and FPGAs (Field Programmable Gate Array), and finally, ASIC (Application-Specific Integrated Circuit) mining.

Initially, all it needed for Bitcoin mining was a simple CPU, and one could become a miner. During that time, it was possible to mine 50 BTC per block with a standard CPU usually present at home. Miners used a standard computer's CPU to perform the mathematical calculations required to verify transactions on a blockchain network.

Since CPUs were designed to handle a wide range of tasks, they were versatile but less efficient for mining cryptocurrencies. Moreover, due to their general-purpose nature, they had a relatively low hash rate and could not perform as many calculations per second as specialized mining hardware. Eventually, they became obsolete for Bitcoin. As the computational difficulty adjustments to mine bitcoins increased, the standard CPUs earlier used were deemed insufficient for mining purposes. Rather, a more robust and efficient processing device was needed. It gave rise to GPU mining and a rapid increase in GPU Hardware costs and demand.

As the name indicates, GPU mining involves using one or more GPU cards to facilitate cryptocurrency mining.[112] GPUs are specialized hardware designed for rendering graphics; they are also well-suited for performing the mathematical calculations required for mining cryptocurrencies. Their ability to handle parallel processing allowed them to perform many calculations simultaneously, making them much more efficient than CPUs for mining. They offered a faster hash processing speed and were typically reserved for mining altcoins. When it came to solving complex problems, GPUs proved to be more efficient and capable than CPUs. Considering their efficiency, they replaced CPUs and became the go-to hardware for cryptocurrency mining. Although they consumed more power than standard CPUs, they still offered worthwhile results in terms of their efficient processing ability. However, over time, the need for computational efficiency increased, and a new solution was needed.

The following years saw a rise in Bitcoin FPGAs and then ASICs among serious miners. ASIC miners are specialized Bitcoin miners who facilitate large Bitcoin mining farms to process transactions and blocks in a very efficient way. They solved the existing inefficiencies in GPU mining and, over time, became the new standard for bitcoin mining. SHA-256 ASICs are specialized hardware designed specifically for mining cryptocurrencies like Bitcoin. They are much more powerful and efficient than CPUs and GPUs for mining. Besides their computational efficiency, ASICs are also more energy-efficient, consuming less power per hash compared to other mining hardware.

The efficiency of ASIC miners comes from the fact that they are specifically designed for Bitcoin mining, unlike CPUs and GPUs, which were not primarily built for this purpose. Since ASICs are designed solely for mining, they might be less versatile than CPUs and GPUs but much more efficient for their intended purpose.

Although they proved to be better than their predecessors in terms of hashing power and energy efficiency, they still consumed significant amounts of energy, which caused miners to begin focusing on creating more efficient mining farms that relied on clean and renewable energy. The aim is to make operations cheaper as well as increase their efficiency. ASIC miners proved themselves to be a breakthrough in the field of cryptocurrency mining, influencing innovation in the field to ensure network security and environmental safety.

On his exploration journey, Roger also learned about the concept of merged mining. He discovered that *"Merged mining refers to the act of mining two or more cryptocurrencies at the same time, without sacrificing overall mining performance.[113]"* This method allows miners to use their computational power to mine blocks on multiple chains concurrently using the Auxiliary Proof of Work (AuxPoW). As a result, a miner can mine two or more blockchains at the same time by solving the cryptographic puzzles for both networks. Intrigued to know more details about this innovative concept, Roger dove deeper into the details to learn how it works. He discovered that merged mining leverages the same computational resources to secure multiple blockchains, allowing miners to contribute to the security of smaller or newer networks without sacrificing their primary mining activities.

In merged mining, the primary blockchain is referred to as the main chain, while the additional blockchains being mined are called auxiliary chains. The main chain's blocks contain information about the auxiliary chain, making it possible to validate both simultaneously. The parent blockchain provides the proof of work, and the auxiliary chain validates it.

The mode of operation revealed the benefits merged mining offers. One of them is increased security, which reduces the risk of a 51% attack. *"It is an attack on a blockchain by a group of miners controlling over 50% of a network's mining hash rate."*[114] Merged mining can enhance the security of auxiliary chains by leveraging the hash power of larger networks. This makes it more difficult for malicious actors to launch 51% attacks on smaller blockchains.

Merged mining allows miners to maximize their computational resources by mining multiple cryptocurrencies simultaneously. This can result in higher profits for miners without the need for additional hardware. It also helps to distribute hash power more evenly across different networks.

(rootstock.io offers merged mining and the launch of smart contracts on the Bitcoin blockchain) As cryptocurrency mining gained traction among individuals, many individual miners tried their luck in cryptocurrency mining. The development of cryptocurrency mining led to solo mining and mining pools. Roger's interest grew in mining, and he began exploring more about it. He discovered that a beginner miner can either begin mining alone or in a group. *Solo mining is the type of cryptocurrency mining where the miner attempts to generate new blocks on his own, with the proceeds from the block reward and transaction fees going entirely to himself, allowing him to receive a large payment with a higher variance (longer time between payments).*[115]

Solo mining involves an individual miner independently managing and executing the mining operations. This means that they do not rely on any third party for any of the operations. Instead of depending on third parties, they leverage the connection with the computers of the native crypto wallet clients to discover wallets and earn rewards.

On the other hand, pool mining is a type of mining where a group of miners pool resources together to find blocks more often collectively. *The mining pools combine the computational power of the connected mining devices.*[116]

When a pool successfully mines a block, the rewards are distributed among the participants based on their contribution to the pool's hash rate. In a mining pool, the coordinator distributes mining tasks to individual miners, who then work on solving these tasks using their computing power. Once a miner in the pool successfully mines a block, it is verified and added to the blockchain. The reward is distributed among the participants, proportional to the amount of hash power contributed by each one of them. This way, miners receive smaller payments but with a lower time variance. The time incurred between the payments is shorter than the time incurred in solo mining. The coordination among mining pools involves hundreds or thousands of miners using specialized pool-mining protocols.

The individual miners configure their mining equipment to connect to a pool server after creating an account with the pool. Their mining hardware remains connected to the pool server while mining, synchronizing their efforts with those of the other miners. Thus, the pool miners share the effort to mine a block and then share in the rewards. *"The pool server will periodically make payments to the miners' Bitcoin addresses once their share of the rewards has reached a certain threshold. Typically, the pool server charges a percentage fee of the rewards for providing the pool-mining service."*[117]

Later on, the mining pools took a more organized form as mining farms arose. *"A mining farm is a mining pool with miners that are housed within a single location and building."* The rise of mining farms has transformed the landscape of cryptocurrency mining, posing both opportunities and challenges for the ecosystem. Mining farms are typically equipped with specialized hardware and infrastructure that can achieve economies of scale that individual miners cannot match—allowing them to mine cryptocurrencies more efficiently and profitably. Moreover, they are often managed by professionals with extensive experience in mining operations, ensuring optimal performance and profitability. Another edge they have over individual miners is the added diversification since mining farms are usually involved in mining multiple cryptocurrencies simultaneously, leveraging diversified portfolios to mitigate risks and maximize returns.

However, they also have their downsides. While mining farms offer economies of scale, professional management, and regulatory compliance, they also raise concerns about centralization, market manipulation, and innovation stagnation. Roger figured out that, as the cryptocurrency ecosystem continues to evolve, finding a balance between mining farms and individual miners will be crucial to ensuring its long-term success and sustainability.

***

One day, while watching a popular TV show, Roger found a reference to Bitcoin.[118] He recalled the time when people hardly knew its name and were skeptical about its worth and future. In just a matter of a few years, it had become an inevitable part of the modern economy and the financial system. However, the growing popularity also meant accelerated regulation efforts by the authorities. After discussions with a few people around him, Roger realized that people widely consider cryptocurrency mining an easy way to make fast money. However, with the development of the other aspects of the market, one crucial aspect that also developed was the financial and regulatory aspects. Cryptocurrency mining rewards do not exclusively belong to miners; instead, they are taxed just like regular income is taxed. It is taxed as income upon receipt.[119] Roger realized that mining cryptocurrency is not only about solving complex mathematical problems or investing in high-performance hardware; it also comes with tax implications that miners need to consider. As with any form of income, the other tax authorities might require miners to report their earnings and pay taxes accordingly.

The mining reward that a miner earns as a result of the successful verification of a transaction and adding a new block to the blockchain is considered taxable income. Upon the disposal of mining rewards, the miner gets a capital loss or gain depending on the current market condition. Even the rewards from the mining pools are taxable income. The miners may need to report their share of the mining income from the pool the pool operator provides. Taxes are not the only thing that miners need to consider before entering the crypto-mining market. Despite the massive popularity of cryptocurrency mining among individuals and companies alike, the path of its development was not free from hurdles.

During his journey to explore cryptocurrency mining, one thing that caught Roger's attention, which he believed many other miners had been overlooking, was the significant environmental impact of mining. The mining process serves two purposes in Bitcoin, including creating new bitcoins in each block and incentivizing miners to include valid transactions in their blocks. A successful miner will collect a reward in the form of new bitcoins and transaction fees. However, the reward will only be collected if the miner has only included valid transactions, with the Bitcoin protocol's rules for consensus determining what is valid. This delicate balance provides security for Bitcoin without a central authority.[120] Although mining achieves a delicate balance between cost and reward, it uses electricity to solve computational problems, which has its environmental impacts. The more advanced the mining hardware got, the higher the potential impact of mining on the environment and exhaustion of resources became. Roger even came across a study that revealed that mining cryptocurrency generates nearly the same amount of CO_2 annually as emitted by a country the size of Greece.[121]

One of the countries showing a firm stance against cryptocurrency mining was China. China's government expressed concerns over the environmental impact and speculative nature of cryptocurrency mining, leading to a crackdown on mining operations in the country. China's ban on mining has caused a significant disruption in the global mining landscape, leading to a drop in the network's hash rate and affecting cryptocurrency prices. However, the impact did not last long.

What shocked Roger was that even after China's ban on cryptocurrency mining, its popularity never declined; instead, it surged. Not only China but eight other countries, including Qatar, Oman, Morocco, Iraq, Egypt, Tunisia, and Algeria, have also banned crypto mining. The impact was nothing else but the increase in the popularity of crypto mining in the US, as most miners who escaped China went to the United States to find better opportunities for crypto mining and cheap energy sources for powering their mining activities. Many Chinese miners relocated their operations to other countries with more favorable regulations and conditions, leading to a redistribution of mining power.

By the time China banned cryptocurrency mining, it had been working as one of the largest cryptocurrency markets, dominating the global cryptocurrency ecosystem. As a result of the ban, the US saw a surge in interest in cryptocurrency mining, with many investors and companies setting up mining farms across the country. Leveraging this opportunity, the US took measures for the growth of crypto mining in the country. Unlike China, the US showed a more supportive stance towards cryptocurrency mining, providing regulatory clarity and incentives for miners. The shift from China to the US and other countries contributed to the decentralization of mining power, reducing the risk of a single country or entity controlling a significant portion of the network's hash rate. It also created new economic opportunities, including job creation and investment in local communities in the United States.

Reflecting on the history and evolution of Bitcoin mining, Roger realized that Bitcoin mining grew each year along with the growth of cryptocurrency and Bitcoin in general. As the popularity of cryptocurrency has surged, so too has the scrutiny surrounding its environmental impact, particularly concerning energy consumption. With traditional mining methods requiring vast amounts of computational power, the ecological footprint of cryptocurrencies like Bitcoin has come under increasing scrutiny. The miners realized that the proof-of-work consensus demands significant computational power, leading to high energy consumption. As the adoption of cryptocurrencies grows, so does their collective energy consumption, raising concerns about sustainability because the energy-intensive nature of mining results in a substantial carbon footprint. Additionally, the rapid turnover of mining hardware leads to electronic waste as outdated or inefficient machines are discarded, further adding to environmental concerns.

The energy consumption and environmental concerns raised by cryptocurrency mining dragged the attention of miners and regulators toward its comparison with traditional banking and financial systems. When he compared traditional banking and gold with cryptocurrency, he was shocked to find out which one among them had the highest energy consumption. The decentralized nature of blockchain networks means that multiple nodes worldwide consume energy to maintain the network. Increasing overall energy consumption does have an impact on the environment and power grids. While traditional banking does not require the same level of energy consumption as cryptocurrency mining, it still has substantial energy demands. This includes powering bank branches, data centers, and ATMs, as well as the energy consumed in printing and transporting physical currency. However, the carbon footprint of cryptocurrency mining has been widely criticized, mainly due to the reliance on fossil fuels in many mining operations. Additionally, the e-waste generated by obsolete mining hardware contributes to environmental degradation.

Despite the alarming figures of energy consumption by cryptocurrency mining, the consumption is still far more economical and efficient than the traditional banking system, which utilizes around 4,981 TWh compared to 120 TWh of Bitcoin. The numbers are nearly 50 times higher when it comes to the legacy banking system.

Even gold mining turns out to be more energy-intensive than Bitcoin, as it stands at around 131 TWh, which is around 10% more than Bitcoin. Moreover, fiat currencies appear less impactful on the environment, considering they can be used several times after creation.[122]

Although the environmental impact of Bitcoin is less than that of its counterparts, it is still not acceptable, and miners and developers are continuously working towards a more energy-efficient and cost-effective solution. In this regard, different efforts have been made by different groups of people and countries. For instance, Japan's largest power production company expressed its idea to turn every unit of its unused electricity into cryptocurrency. This involves the concept of putting alternating current to use. However, it also has a downside: the alternative current generated at the power plant is supplied through wires and transformers to every user. However, this does not ensure the correct adjustment of the output to the actual demand. Due to this, a significant amount of energy is often wasted. Bitcoin miners can make a difference by utilizing surplus energy to fuel their mining activity and reducing waste.

When he looked at the various energy sources used by Bitcoin miners, he discovered that the major energy source for Bitcoin mining is hydropower. However, considering the situation of cryptocurrency mining, various miners have resorted to alternate energy sources. For instance, he learned about a company in Pennsylvania that uses waste coal to fuel Bitcoin mining.[123] They realized the environmental hazards posed by waste coal piles in their area. They decided to put them to better use by turning the waste coal into electricity in specialized power plants and using it to mine cryptocurrencies.

Moreover, the older fossil-fuel power plants that were shut down earlier in favor of renewable energy gained a second life as Bitcoin miners began using them. A switch towards energy-efficient alternatives and new developments took place in the cryptocurrency ecosystem. For instance, the Proof of Stake mechanism was introduced as an alternative to the PoW mechanism. PoS is a more energy-efficient alternative to PoW, requiring significantly less computational power and, therefore, consuming less energy.[124] This led to a shift from cryptocurrency mining to staking. While mining validates transactions by using powerful computers and consuming significant energy, staking adopts a more energy-efficient approach. It involves validating transactions by holding tokens and ultimately using less energy than mining. The shift from traditional mining to staking emerged as a more energy-efficient and sustainable alternative for maintaining blockchain networks.

Roger observed two of the most noteworthy examples of transition: Ethereum (ETH) and Polygon (MATIC). These cryptocurrencies transitioned from proof-of-work (PoW) mining to proof-of-stake (PoS) consensus mechanisms. Unlike PoW, where miners compete to solve complex mathematical puzzles to validate transactions and add new blocks to the blockchain, PoS relies on validators who lock up a certain amount of their cryptocurrency as a "stake" to participate in the consensus process. Validators are chosen to create new blocks based on their stake and the age of their holdings rather than computational power.

As a part of these efforts, Roger witnessed a transition from staking to yield farming, *a high-risk, volatile investment strategy where an investor stakes, or lends, crypto assets on a decentralized finance (DeFi) platform to earn a higher return.*[125] Although all three methods facilitate cryptocurrency investment, the preference among these methods depends on individual factors such as technical expertise, up-front costs, and environmental concerns. Ethereum, the second-largest cryptocurrency by market capitalization, is undergoing a major upgrade known as Ethereum 2.0, which includes a transition from PoW to PoS. The Beacon Chain, the first phase of Ethereum 2.0, was launched in December 2020, marking the beginning of the transition to a more scalable and sustainable network. The transition to Ethereum 2.0 aims to address scalability issues, reduce energy consumption, and lower transaction fees.

By leveraging PoS, Ethereum 2.0 aims to achieve greater network efficiency and environmental sustainability while maintaining decentralization and security. Polygon, initially known as Matic Network, was designed with a PoS consensus mechanism from its inception. This architecture allows Polygon to offer fast and low-cost transactions, making it an attractive platform for decentralized applications (dApps) and DeFi projects. The PoS consensus mechanism of Polygon contributes to its efficiency and scalability, facilitating the development of innovative solutions across various sectors. Luckily, the transition to staking coins like ETH and Polygon has the potential to significantly reduce the environmental impact associated with cryptocurrency mining. By eliminating the need for energy-intensive mining rigs, staking contributes to a more sustainable blockchain ecosystem. Staking offers cryptocurrency holders an alternative investment opportunity, offering potential returns through staking rewards. This financial incentive encourages participation in network validation and contributes to the overall security and decentralization of the blockchain.

Looking back at cryptocurrency mining, Roger knew that earlier, it was a lucrative business, without question. However, considering the massive change in the market and overall industry, he had to consider it with a bit more concern to decide if cryptocurrency mining would be profitable in the recent year. He decided to get an expert opinion about it and consulted an expert miner in the field to discuss the potential of cryptocurrency mining in 2024.

"Nowadays, the profitability of crypto mining depends on the type of cryptocurrency you choose to mine. Although Bitcoin is still one of the most profitable cryptocurrencies to mine, its mining difficulty has significantly increased in recent years. Therefore, it might not be as viable for individual miners as it is for pool miners.

I would suggest you look into other cryptocurrencies like Ethereum, Litecoin, Monero, Bitcoin Cash, and Zcash. Since they have a different algorithm than Bitcoin, they are comparatively easier to mine. They also have potential for future growth, making them ideal for beginners. However, keep in mind that the profitability of mining these coins depends on their mining difficulty, hardware and power costs, and market value."

He also shared some worthwhile mining strategies and tips that might help maximize miners' profits. He advised Roger to utilize the correct mining hardware, such as GPUs and ASICs, as it impacts the overall mining experience and profits. Using cost-effective energy sources is also crucial to decreasing costs and increasing profits.

"The best strategy is to consider pool mining, as it allows you to combine your mining resources with those of other miners and leverage them to maximize your mining potential with more frequent but reduced rewards."

Roger discovered that a recent practice gaining traction among modern-time miners was cloud mining, which involves renting mining hardware from a cloud-based service provider and using it to mine different cryptocurrencies. Despite being more expensive, this option tends to be more profitable. Roger's research revealed to him that despite the massive transformation of the cryptocurrency mining landscape, there are still opportunities if one figures out the right approach and invests time in keeping up with market trends. Before entering the increasingly competitive cryptocurrency mining industry, an individual must consider factors such as access to cheap electricity, mining hardware, mining options, associated risks, and cost-benefit analysis compared to retail purchasing, holding, and staking, if applicable.

Chapter 9: The Future of Cryptocurrency

When Bitcoin was launched in 2009, nobody, including Roger, knew what it held for the financial system and the transformation of the existing monetary system. However, after a decade of its journey, it revealed so many aspects of its development and growth that Roger could now make calculated predictions about the future of cryptocurrency. Based on market news and predictions, he knew that the future of cryptocurrency is highly dynamic and subject to various factors, such as technological advancements, regulatory frameworks, and global economic trends. However, some key aspects can be highlighted to provide insight into the potential trajectory of this digital asset class. As more individuals and institutions recognize the potential of cryptocurrencies for faster, cheaper, and more secure transactions, adoption rates are expected to grow further. The popularity of Ordinals (Bitcoin NFTs) and other novel use cases of cryptocurrency speaks volumes of the inclination of people toward cryptocurrency as the foundation of a decentralized economy. This could lead to greater mainstream acceptance and broader usage, driving the overall value of these digital assets.

One significant factor shaping cryptocurrency's future is the development of clear and consistent regulatory frameworks across different jurisdictions. This would provide a stable environment for businesses and investors, fostering growth and innovation in the industry. The continuous evolution of blockchain technology and the emergence of new cryptocurrencies, such as those based on proof-of-stake consensus mechanisms (Ethereum, Solana, Toncoin, Cardano, and Avalanche), could lead to more efficient and environmentally sustainable digital assets. Additionally, advancements in scalability solutions, smart contract functionality, and interoperability between different blockchains may further enhance the usability and appeal of cryptocurrencies. As more financial institutions and corporations begin to invest in and adopt cryptocurrencies, the overall credibility and legitimacy of the asset class will increase. The greater the institutional investment, the further it will drive up the value of cryptocurrencies and attract more retail investors.

Stablecoins, which are cryptocurrencies pegged to stable assets like fiat currencies or commodities, are expected to play a crucial role in providing price stability and facilitating transactions. The Central Bank Digital Currencies, on the other hand, could potentially disrupt the financial landscape by offering a digital form of fiat currency with the benefits of blockchain technology. Moreover, the growth of decentralized finance (DeFi) platforms and non-fungible tokens (NFTs) has shown the potential for innovative use cases of blockchain technology. These developments could lead to new business models and financial instruments, further expanding the utility and value of cryptocurrencies. Despite all the developments going on in the crypto space and the concerns about its future, its potential remains unparalleled, with predictions that the market will reach $25 trillion by 2030.[126] This hints that cryptocurrency is likely to endure, continuing its growth trajectory to address scalability and security issues and offer viable investment opportunities to individuals. Similarly, the regulatory developments in the industry are expected to contribute to enhancing the accessibility of Bitcoin and other cryptocurrencies, which can prove to be a regulatory breakthrough in their growth as digital assets.

On April 20, 2024, he saw the news about the completion of the fourth Bitcoin halving.[127] Although Bitcoin halving is often associated with a surge in its price, the recent halving event resulted in the price of Bitcoin holding steady at about $63,907. He also discovered that the next halving event is expected to occur somewhere in mid-2028 when the network reaches a block height of 1,050,000. Recalling the halving phenomenon, Roger remembered that the preprogrammed event of Bitcoin halving occurs every four years to regulate Bitcoin production and ensure its limited supply. When the reward for Bitcoin mining is cut in half, the number of bitcoins entering the market also reduces, keeping the supply of the coins regulated compared with market demand. As a result of the fourth halving that recently happened, the Bitcoin mining reward was reduced from 6.25 Bitcoins to 3.125 coins. This reward will be further reduced (halved) in the next halving event, which will probably happen in mid-2028.

Out of the 21 million bitcoins that will ever exist in the cryptocurrency ecosystem, around 19.5 million have already been mined, leaving only around 1.3 million coins to be mined.[128] As long as the demand remains constant, bitcoin prices are expected to rise in response to the halving. However, the study of historical data revealed that the impact of Bitcoin halving its price is not fixed. The price may not increase soon after the halving impact, but it may take some time to reflect the impact of the change. The earlier three halving events showed a similar pattern when the prices showed an impact a year after the halving events. After the July 2016 halving, prices quadrupled in a year, whereas the May 2020 halving witnessed a seven-times increase in prices a year later. However, in the ever-evolving cryptocurrency world, past performances cannot be considered an indicator of future results.

Roger thought about the impact of the halving on miners. Since the mining rewards are halved, the miners are challenged to reduce the mining costs and adjust them to their reduced income. Unless there is a sharp increase in bitcoin's price, miners would have a challenging time adjusting their expenditures within a fixed income. Experts have different views about whether or not the price rise will occur. Nothing, but the future can reveal what it holds for Bitcoin miners.

Despite the tremendous growth of cryptocurrencies, Roger knew that the path was not free from obstacles. One of the foremost among them is regulatory uncertainty. Cryptocurrencies operate in a regulatory environment that varies across countries and jurisdictions. The lack of clear and consistent global regulation can lead to legal ambiguity, hindering the adoption and growth of digital assets. Cryptocurrency platforms and exchanges are vulnerable to cyberattacks, which can result in significant financial losses for users. Ensuring the security of digital assets and implementing robust security measures will remain a critical challenge for the industry. As cryptocurrency users grow, so does the need for faster and more efficient transactions. Blockchain networks, particularly those with slower processing times and high transaction fees, may struggle to keep up with demand, potentially limiting the mass adoption of certain cryptocurrencies. Proof-of-work consensus mechanisms, commonly used by cryptocurrencies like Bitcoin, require substantial energy resources.

The environmental impact of these energy-intensive processes has raised concerns among policymakers and the public, potentially leading to regulatory restrictions or public backlash against cryptocurrencies.[129] Cryptocurrencies are known for their volatile prices, which can deter potential investors and users. Price stability is crucial for widespread adoption, and efforts to mitigate volatility through stablecoins, improved market infrastructure, and increased institutional involvement are ongoing. While some banks and financial institutions are exploring cryptocurrencies and blockchain technology, widespread adoption remains limited.

Overcoming resistance and integrating cryptocurrencies into traditional financial systems will be a significant challenge. Many people still lack a comprehensive understanding of cryptocurrencies and their potential benefits and risks. Increasing public awareness and providing accessible educational resources will be essential for responsible adoption and investment decisions. As the cryptocurrency landscape evolves, new digital assets and blockchain platforms will continue to emerge, challenging the dominance of established cryptocurrencies like Bitcoin and Ethereum. Staying competitive and adapting to the latest innovations will be crucial for the future success of existing cryptocurrencies.

Cryptocurrencies are influenced by global economic trends and geopolitical events, which can impact their adoption, regulation, and overall market sentiment. Navigating these challenges will require adaptability and strategic planning from industry participants and policymakers alike. In Roger's opinion, integrating cryptocurrencies into daily transactions and financial systems would be crucial for widespread adoption.

This integration would require collaboration between governments, financial institutions, and the cryptocurrency industry to establish clear regulatory frameworks, improve the user experience, and ensure security and stability. However, some key aspects need to be addressed. Governments and regulatory bodies need to develop clear and consistent guidelines for cryptocurrency usage, covering areas such as anti-money laundering (AML), know-your-customer (KYC) procedures, taxation, and consumer protection. These frameworks should strike a balance between fostering innovation and ensuring the stability and security of financial systems. Moreover, cryptocurrencies should be compatible with existing financial infrastructure, such as banking systems and payment networks, to facilitate seamless integration with the existing financial system. This can be achieved through partnerships between cryptocurrency companies and traditional financial institutions and the development of interoperability standards and protocols.

Cryptocurrencies can become more accessible to the general public by improving user interfaces and simplifying the onboarding process. This includes developing intuitive wallets, exchanges, and payment platforms catering to tech-savvy users and those with limited experience in the space. Education and awareness campaigns can also help demystify cryptocurrencies and encourage their adoption. Cryptocurrencies need to address scalability issues and improve transaction speeds to handle high transaction volumes and support daily use cases. Advancements in blockchain technology, such as layer-2 solutions, sharding, and off-chain transactions, can help to achieve this. As mentioned earlier, stablecoins can significantly promote financial stability and encourage widespread cryptocurrency adoption. By pegging cryptocurrencies to stable assets, stablecoins can provide users with a more predictable store of value, making them suitable for everyday transactions and financial systems.

A successful integration of cryptocurrencies into daily transactions and financial systems requires collaboration between traditional financial institutions and the cryptocurrency industry. This collaboration can lead to innovative solutions, such as developing a digital wallet. Crypto firms can bridge the gap with traditional finance by addressing key challenges, fostering collaboration, and implementing innovative solutions. As he heard about the US Securities and Exchange Commission's (SEC) scrutiny of many digital currencies and unregistered securities, he couldn't help but think about its impact on the ever-evolving digital currency landscape. He knew the approval of retirement accounts adding Bitcoin Exchange-Traded Funds (ETFs) by the Securities and Exchange Commission (SEC) would be a significant milestone for the cryptocurrency industry.[130] This development could potentially bring Bitcoin and other digital assets closer to mainstream adoption, providing everyday people with a more accessible way to invest in cryptocurrencies.

A Bitcoin ETF listed on major stock exchanges would allow everyday investors to gain exposure to Bitcoin through their retirement accounts, such as Individual Retirement Accounts (IRAs). This would provide a more regulated and familiar investment vehicle compared to directly purchasing and storing cryptocurrencies. The approval of a Bitcoin ETF would also require the SEC to ensure that the fund meets strict regulatory requirements, providing an additional layer of investor protection. This would help mitigate some of the risks associated with investing in cryptocurrencies, potentially attracting a more comprehensive range of investors.

The approval of a Bitcoin ETF could lead to increased institutional investment in cryptocurrencies. Asset managers, pension funds, and other institutional investors may find investing in a regulated and familiar investment vehicle like an ETF more appealing than directly dealing with the complexities of cryptocurrencies. This increased institutional investment could also help improve the liquidity of the Bitcoin market, reducing price volatility and providing a more stable environment for retail investors.

The SEC-approved Bitcoin ETF is undoubtedly increasing the legitimacy of cryptocurrencies in the eyes of the general public and financial institutions. This increased legitimacy could lead to broader mainstream adoption, further driving the growth and development of the cryptocurrency industry. The approved Bitcoin ETF could bring numerous benefits, but there are also potential challenges and considerations. These include concerns about market manipulation, price volatility, and the need for robust regulatory frameworks to protect investors.

The SEC's approval of retirement accounts adding Bitcoin ETFs would be a significant step toward the mainstream adoption of cryptocurrencies. This development could increase accessibility, attract institutional investors, and enhance the legitimacy of digital assets. However, it is essential to address potential challenges and ensure that appropriate regulatory frameworks are in place to protect investors and maintain market integrity.

While observing the latest trends in the cryptocurrency market, Roger found that speculations about CBDC also entered the market, where some consider it to be the perfect alternative to cryptocurrencies despite the many downsides they possess. *"A central bank digital currency (CBDC) is a form of digital currency issued by a country's central bank. It is similar to cryptocurrencies, except that its value is fixed by the central bank and is equivalent to the country's fiat currency."[131]*

Many countries that have realized the significance of switching to digital currencies are working to develop CBDC. CBDCs might appear similar to other digital currencies or cryptocurrencies; however, there is a stark difference between the two. The most important thing that differentiates CBDC from cryptocurrencies is its control and authority. Unlike cryptocurrencies, CBDCs are issued and controlled by the central bank. This means that just as the paper fiat currency is the liability of the central bank, so are CBDCs.

CBDCs are issued and regulated by central banks, whereas cryptocurrencies like Bitcoin are not backed or regulated by any central authority. This difference in issuance leads to distinct governance structures and decision-making processes. Moreover, there is a difference in the stability of both currencies. CBDCs are generally pegged to the value of the country's fiat currency, providing perceived stability and reducing the risk of volatility associated with cryptocurrencies. On the other hand, cryptocurrencies can experience significant price fluctuations due to market demand and supply dynamics. The main objective behind the development of CBDCs is to improve the efficiency and effectiveness of a country's existing payment systems and financial infrastructure. Cryptocurrencies, like Bitcoin, often aim to disrupt traditional financial systems and promote decentralization, challenging the role of central banks and governments in managing the money supply and monetary policy. Most cryptocurrencies, including Bitcoin, offer users a certain level of anonymity, making it more difficult to trace transactions. CBDCs, however, can be designed to be more traceable, even evasive, allowing central banks and governments to monitor transactions for purposes such as combating money laundering, tax evasion, and financing terrorism. While both CBDCs and cryptocurrencies can leverage blockchain or distributed ledger technology, the specific implementations and use cases may differ.[132] CBDCs can be designed to operate on permissioned blockchains (vs. permissionless) or other distributed ledger systems, providing more control and security while still maintaining the benefits of digital transactions.

Despite being digital currencies, CBDCs and cryptocurrencies like Bitcoin differ in terms of issuance, regulation, stability, purpose, anonymity, and technology. CBDCs are designed to complement and improve existing financial systems, while cryptocurrencies often seek to challenge and disrupt them.

Roger read a forecast that by 2028, only 9% of transactions will take place using physical currency. The rest of the transactions would be digitalized. However, for Roger, digital cash replacement seems like an uphill task.

He thought, *"What if the core structures of our financial world were on the verge of a paradigm shift with the rise of Central Bank Digital Currencies (CBDCs)?"* He knew that a CBDC represents a legal tender that can be used for various transactions, similar to physical cash but in a digital format. These currencies are designed to coexist with a country's existing payment systems and traditional fiat currency to provide benefits such as increased efficiency, cost reduction, and financial inclusion. Roger found that a significant step forward towards the centralization and digitalization of the monetary system was the Chinese social credit system.

The Social Credit System (SCS) in China is a government-backed initiative aimed at evaluating and rating the behavior and trustworthiness of individuals and organizations. The social credit system of China is a crucial part of the Chinese socialist economic market system. *It is based on laws, regulations, standards, and contracts and covers a network of credit records and credit infrastructure for members of society.*[133] The credit system is inspired by the concept of a "social credit score," which is similar to the one portrayed in the famous Netflix show Black Mirror episode "Nosedive." In this anthology TV series, each episode presents an altered reality, focusing on various real-world aspects. The episode "Nosedive" discusses how the world would be if social media were used to define people's actual worth. The episode presents a rating mechanism through which people rate each other. The rating plays a significant role in individuals' lives, affecting various aspects, from their work to their social life. Once the protagonist loses her rating, she faces a trail of challenges in her personal and professional life and eventually ends up in prison.

The Chinese Social Credit System also presents a similar framework and affects people's lives. A person's social credit score can influence their access to various services, such as loans, credit cards, and insurance. Those with a higher score may receive better interest rates and more favorable terms, while those with a lower score may face restrictions or be denied access to these services altogether. Some employers and educational institutions in China have started using the social credit score as a factor in hiring and admissions decisions. Individuals with a higher score may have better chances of getting hired or admitted, while those with a lower score may face difficulties in these areas.

The social credit system can also impact an individual's ability to travel domestically and internationally. For example, people with a low score may be restricted from buying high-speed train tickets or taking flights.[134] Additionally, those who violate traffic laws may face penalties, such as being banned from driving or taking public transportation. A low social credit score and its resulting impacts can lead to social stigma and a damaged reputation, as people may perceive those with a lower score as less trustworthy or responsible. This can impact personal and professional relationships, as well as opportunities for networking and social interactions.

In some cases, a low social credit score can lead to legal consequences, such as fines, demotions, or even criminal prosecution.[135] For example, businesses with low scores may face penalties, and individuals who repeatedly violate social norms or engage in fraudulent activities may face legal repercussions. Due to these characteristics, the Chinese Social Credit System is often compared with the fictional portrayal in "Nosedive." Although the system aims to promote social harmony, responsibility, and trustworthiness, it also raises concerns about privacy, freedom, and potential abuses of power.

One thing that Roger deduced after his research about the ongoing progress for the implementation of digital cash and the Chinese credit system was that it brings the dangers of control to individuals and threatens individual freedom. The dangers of control for a person can manifest in various ways, affecting their mental, emotional, and physical well-being. When individuals are subjected to excessive control, they may lose their ability to make financial decisions and control their lives independently. This can lead to feelings of powerlessness, low self-esteem, and a lack of confidence in their abilities.

Many experts have also discussed the threat of reduced financial freedom that the CBDC carries. It may also lead to a social chilling effect where individuals are afraid of engaging in the expression of their ideas for fear of strict laws and regulations. Excessive control can suppress an individual's creativity and self-expression, as they may feel the need to conform to the expectations and preferences of those in power. This can limit their personal growth and hinder their ability to explore new ideas and perspectives.

He tried to imagine a day in which a Central Bank Digital Currency (CBDC) controls various aspects of an individual's life to understand the pros and cons of this system. He visualized that he might wake up with the intelligent alarm clock linked to his CBDC and get freshly brewed morning coffee through his CBDC-linked coffee machine. In the event of insufficient funds in his account, he might not be able to get his morning coffee, and neither would his alarm ring. The same mechanism governs your smart fridge, which only contains healthy food items. Poor dietary choices may lead to a lower CBDC score, which might ultimately lock in unhealthy food choices. Similarly, his commute, performance at work, meals, taxes, entertainment, and other aspects of life may follow a similar pattern. This would bring its own set of few advantages and many downsides that are yet to be discovered.

As Roger took a deep dive into the forecasts and speculations, he discovered that the development of a similar social credit system was in progress in the USA. The related theories also indicated that the potential scope of the soft social credit system under construction is enormous.[136] Under this system, companies would be able to track individuals' activities and give them corporate rewards or punishments that could block transactions, add surcharges, or even restrict the use of certain products. People even believe that the CBDCs would mark an end to American freedom.[137] However, Roger knew that the reality would only become clear once the digital monetary system came into existence or the idea so incompatible with American liberty and constitutional rights that it could be banned before it had a chance to exist. (The CBDC Anti-Surveillance State Act was introduced in both US congressional chambers as of Feb 2024, which prohibits the FED from creating a CBDC. The US House passed the resolution in May 2024)

After his long but worthwhile journey in the cryptocurrency ecosystem, Roger could see how it might affect the future of the monetary system. Statistics revealed that nearly 2 billion payments made across the world are digital every day, and Roger could see a burst of creative innovation underway in the monetary system.[138] He anticipated that more avenues for a digital monetary system would open up in the future, facilitating the creation of a robust digital monetary system. However, the role of cryptocurrency in founding the basis of the future monetary system was yet to be decided. The structural flaws in the crypto universe and some other downsides of this ecosystem make it unsuitable for a scalable digital monetary system. The reliance on cryptocurrency by unregulated intermediaries also poses several financial risks.

On the other hand, a system based on central bank money sounds more suitable for the creation and development of a monetary system that would have room for innovation and scalability. He also believed that the capabilities usually associated with the cryptocurrency ecosystem, such as programmability, composability, and tokenization, could not be built on CBDCs. Roger remembers that "Bitcoin was created during the financial crash of 2008 because of the low trust in banking institutions and the FED. It also was conceived to give more transactional freedom and the ability for an individual to store monetary value without the permission or control of a central authority." In his opinion, the future of the monetary system is likely to be shaped by several key factors and trends, including the rise in the crypto market cap, advancements in financial technology, increasing globalization pressure, and growing concerns around financial freedom and privacy. Central banks and financial institutions will likely play a more significant role in promoting investments in nuclear power, power infrastructure, and clean coal. Although the impact of cryptocurrency on the future monetary system is yet to be decided, its money-making potential for investors is undeniable.

Roger concluded that after a decade of massive transformation and evolution in the cryptocurrency space, the future of cryptocurrency as an investment looks bright. The approval of the spot Bitcoin exchange-traded-fund (ETF) and novel use cases of cryptocurrency have added to the optimism around its growth potential.[139] Moreover, the massive transformation and technological development in the cryptocurrency sphere hint towards a brighter future of blockchain technology and its supporting network.

Amidst the abundance of speculations and predictions of cryptocurrency, one thing remains clear: the Bitcoin blockchain will continue to improve in terms of scalability and security. Crypto and Bitcoin will remain a subject of great interest for investors and remain in the spotlight among speculators. Bitcoin and other cryptocurrencies are likely to remain popular with a specific group of risk-tolerant investors. At the same time, the future of the monetary systems would likely be built upon a combination of different technologies and digital innovations.

Chapter 10: Conclusion

Roger's journey through the complicated landscape of cryptocurrency depicts the journey of various other crypto enthusiasts and programmers who witnessed the massive transformation of digital currency from its inception to cryptocurrency dominating the financial and monetary system.

On his journey to explore the voyage of Bitcoin and cryptocurrency, Roger uncovered a series of fascinating narratives of innovation, creativity, modernization, and transformative potential. Roger, who entered this space out of curiosity, could not help but dive deeper into it and experience its prospective opportunities first-hand. Each chapter of this book helped you have a closer look at Roger's journey to develop a keen understanding of this ecosystem and comprehend the dynamics that rule this industry. Highlighting the 15 years since the Bitcoin whitepaper was released and the first blockchain came online, Roger covered his journey and reflection over those years. Beginning from Bitcoin's complicated origins to achieving various evolutionary milestones that ultimately shaped the landscape of this groundbreaking digital asset.

Exchanging thousands of Bitcoins for a couple of pizzas might seem like a laughable idea today. Still, as mentioned in Chapter Two, when Laszlo Hanyecz offered ten thousand Bitcoins in exchange for two pizzas, no one seemed interested in that offer. People initially did not even believe it, and those who even believed it did not seem to be interested in it unless someone accepted the offer. This led to the famous Bitcoin pizza transaction, which became a historic trademark in Bitcoin history. The inception of Bitcoin, often shrouded in mystery under the pseudonym of Satoshi Nakamoto, marked a pivotal moment in the history of financial system development. Emerging in the aftermath of the 2008 financial crisis, Bitcoin was envisioned as a decentralized currency free from the shackles of traditional financial institutions. Despite presenting an ideal solution to the existing problems in the financial and monetary systems, the currency initially suffered a lack of trust from its users for the right reasons. With the aftereffects of the 2008 financial crisis still evident, trusting the novel idea of a decentralized currency was hard to swallow. However, this did not prevent the potential of cryptocurrency from realizing its array of possibilities. As discussed in the first chapter, Satoshi Nakamoto laid the groundwork for a peer-to-peer electronic cash system that would disrupt the status quo through cryptographic principles and blockchain technology.

The blockchain technology and network discussed by Satoshi Nakamoto in his Bitcoin whitepaper soon became the talk of the town with the blockchain revolution. Central to the saga of Bitcoin is the revolutionary blockchain technology that underpins its operations. Blockchain, a distributed ledger system, enables transparent, immutable, and secure transactions, ushering in a new era of trustless peer-to-peer interactions. As explained in the second chapter, the blockchain's decentralized nature promised to empower individuals with unprecedented control over their financial assets, transcending geographical boundaries and intermediaries. However, the early years of adoption and usage of Bitcoin were marked by several challenges, including limited public awareness and experimental use cases. After slow growth in the early years, the user base and transaction volume gradually gained momentum. As a result of the growing awareness, more people became interested in Bitcoin mining but were unaware of the framework to follow for entering this world.

Moreover, the concentration of Bitcoin mining in the hands of a few individuals raised concerns about centralization and potential manipulation. These concerns were eradicated over time as mining pools emerged, distributing power and increasing network security. After going through various stages of trials, errors, developments, and innovation, cryptocurrency, which initially started as a mere concept, finally became a global phenomenon. The journey of Bitcoin and cryptocurrency from a mere concept to a global phenomenon speaks volumes about human ingenuity, resilience, and the relentless pursuit of innovation. What began as an abstract idea discussed and speculated on the confines of a white paper thrived into a transformative force reshaping the landscape of finance and technology on a global scale.

Initially, Bitcoin emerged as a hope for a departure from the downsides of traditional financial systems, challenging the ultimate control of centralized authorities and intermediaries. The visionaries behind this disruptive technology have probably envisioned a world where individuals could transact seamlessly without the need for third-party oversight. It appeared to be the perfect solution to the pitfalls of the centralized monetary system and inflation. After the initial uncertainty among the public turned into growing interest, the concept gained traction within niche circles, leading cryptocurrency enthusiasts and early adopters to explore the secrets of the decentralized currency and let the world know about it. The community of early developers, miners, and advocates laid the groundwork for a burgeoning ecosystem characterized by experimentation, innovation, and occasional setbacks. Despite initial skepticism and regulatory hurdles, the resilience of the cryptocurrency community propelled Bitcoin into the mainstream consciousness.

Over time, various alternative cryptocurrencies and innovative use cases of blockchain technology also became a part of the crypto ecosystem. From decentralized finance (DeFi) platforms reimagining traditional banking services to non-fungible tokens (NFTs) revolutionizing digital ownership, various innovations proved the transformative potential of this technology. Amidst the battle between challenges and opportunities, cryptocurrencies continued their growth trajectory, ultimately becoming a global phenomenon.

The evolution of Bitcoin from obscurity to prominence catalyzed a broader renaissance in digital finance, paving the way for a diverse array of cryptocurrencies and blockchain-based applications. From Ethereum's introduction of smart contracts to the growth of decentralized exchanges and digital assets, the cryptocurrency landscape soon developed into a vibrant ecosystem with a broad scope for creativity and possibility. At the same time, the global embrace of cryptocurrencies transcended geographical boundaries, fostering a borderless community united by a shared vision of financial sovereignty and empowerment. As individuals across the globe leveraged cryptocurrencies to avoid financial barriers, preserve wealth, and participate in novel forms of economic activity, the phenomenon became global.

However, the rise of Bitcoin and cryptocurrency from anonymity to ubiquity has not been without its challenges. Regulatory scrutiny, market volatility, and technological bottlenecks have posed formidable obstacles along the path to mass adoption. Similarly, it has also become a popular tool among scammers and hackers. As discussed in Chapter Four in detail, various cryptocurrency exchanges became targets of scammers, leading to massive losses among investors. Yet, with each trial and tribulation, the resilience of the cryptocurrency community prevailed, driving innovation and propelling the industry forward.

At the forefront of the cryptocurrency revolution stands Decentralized finance (DeFi), which has the potential to revolutionize the way we conceive and interact with traditional financial services. The trends and speculations hint that the allure of decentralized finance is ready to captivate an ever-expanding audience, leading to a massive transformation in the financial landscape. At its core, DeFi represents a paradigm shift in the provision of financial services, leveraging blockchain technology to bypass intermediaries and facilitate peer-to-peer transactions in a trustless manner. From lending and borrowing to trading and asset management, the scope of DeFi applications is as diverse as it is revolutionary, offering users unprecedented autonomy, transparency, and efficiency.

One of the primary drivers behind the growing popularity of DeFi is its promise of financial inclusion. By removing barriers to entry and democratizing access to financial services, DeFi empowers individuals across the globe to participate in an open and inclusive financial ecosystem, irrespective of geographical location or socioeconomic status. From unbanked individuals in developing war-torn countries to underbanked communities in the developed world, DeFi represents hope for those marginalized by traditional financial systems, offering a lifeline to financial empowerment and economic agency.

Moreover, the allure of DeFi lies in its potential to revolutionize traditional banking services and offer users a viable alternative to centralized financial institutions. By harnessing the power of smart contracts and decentralized networks, DeFi protocols facilitate seamless peer-to-peer lending and borrowing, enabling users to earn interest on their assets or access liquidity without the need for intermediaries.

This disintermediation of traditional banking services not only reduces costs and inefficiencies but also fosters greater financial autonomy and control for users. If we look closely, the future of DeFi appears inexorably linked with the broader evolution of cryptocurrency and blockchain technology. With each passing day, DeFi protocols are becoming increasingly sophisticated, interoperable, and user-friendly, lowering barriers to entry and expanding the reach of decentralized finance to new audiences. Moreover, the convergence of DeFi with emerging technologies such as artificial intelligence, the Internet of Things (IoT), and decentralized autonomous organizations (DAOs) promises to unlock new frontiers of possibility, fostering innovation and collaboration on a scale previously unimaginable.

Besides DeFi, another digital asset innovation with considerable growth potential is altcoins. These alternatives to Bitcoin are believed to possess the potential to offer considerable returns to investors, which may overtake Bitcoin's investment returns.[140] With their potential to be occasionally less volatile than Bitcoin, they are considered to be a lucrative investment option. Various altcoins offer certain benefits over Bitcoin, such as better speed and lower processing fees. These factors make them a likely option to dominate the cryptocurrency market and even compete with the most popular cryptocurrency, Bitcoin.

Altcoins, alternative cryptocurrencies to Bitcoin, have emerged as dynamic contenders within the cryptocurrency landscape. They tend to have the potential to capture a greater market share and redefine the contours of digital finance. These diverse digital assets are primed to ascend to new heights of popularity and utility in the future. The appeal of altcoins lies in their capacity to innovate upon the foundational principles established by Bitcoin, offering unique features, functionalities, and use cases tailored to meet the diverse needs of users and investors. One of the primary drivers behind the growing popularity of altcoins is their potential for diversification and portfolio optimization. While Bitcoin remains the preeminent cryptocurrency by market capitalization and mainstream recognition, altcoins offer investors a broader spectrum of investment opportunities spanning various sectors, industries, and technological paradigms.

By strategically allocating capital across a diversified portfolio of altcoins, investors can mitigate risk, capitalize on emerging trends, and potentially enhance returns in an ever-evolving market landscape. Moreover, the proliferation of altcoins has democratized access to financial services and investment opportunities, empowering individuals around the world to participate in the burgeoning digital economy. From decentralized finance (DeFi) platforms enabling lending, borrowing, and yield farming to non-fungible tokens (NFTs) revolutionizing digital ownership and content monetization, altcoins serve as enablers of innovation and disruption across diverse verticals, transcending traditional boundaries and intermediaries.

The transformative development of cryptocurrency underscored the significance of understanding this landscape and staying informed about the latest happenings in this ecosystem. As cryptocurrencies continue to permeate mainstream discourse and reshape global markets, individuals, businesses, and policymakers alike are faced with the challenge of adapting to the changing scenarios in the financial world. Unlike traditional fiat currencies, which are governed by centralized authorities, cryptocurrencies operate on decentralized networks secured by cryptographic algorithms. This fundamental departure from the status quo introduces a host of unique opportunities and challenges that demand a clear understanding to navigate effectively. For individuals, understanding cryptocurrency extends beyond mere financial literacy to personal empowerment. By familiarizing themselves with the underlying technologies and principles driving cryptocurrencies, individuals can seize control of their financial destinies, mitigate risks, and capitalize on emerging opportunities in the digital economy. Whether as a means of diversifying investment portfolios, facilitating cross-border transactions, or participating in decentralized finance (DeFi) platforms, cryptocurrency proficiency empowers individuals to navigate an increasingly digitized world with confidence and agency.

Businesses, too, stand to reap substantial benefits from a comprehensive understanding of cryptocurrency. From startups leveraging blockchain technology to optimize supply chain management to established enterprises exploring tokenization and decentralized governance structures, cryptocurrency proficiency unlocks a range of avenues for innovation, efficiency, and competitive advantage. By staying abreast of emerging trends and regulatory developments in the cryptocurrency space, businesses can position themselves at the vanguard of industry disruption, ready to capitalize on the transformative potential of digital finance. Moreover, policymakers and regulatory bodies play a pivotal role in shaping the trajectory of cryptocurrency adoption and integration within broader socio-economic frameworks. Informed decision-making and proactive engagement with stakeholders are essential to foster an environment conducive to innovation, consumer protection, and market stability.

By fostering dialogue, conducting thorough risk assessments, and implementing robust regulatory frameworks that balance innovation and freedom with investor safeguards, policymakers can harness the potential of cryptocurrency to drive economic growth, foster financial inclusion, and promote social equity.

The best strategy to stay updated with the latest cryptocurrency news and updates is to set personalized alerts on your devices. Various news platforms offer personalized updates to help you stay updated with market news, trends, and the latest updates regarding your specific cryptocurrencies. Moreover, engaging in cryptocurrency communities and discussion platforms can make a huge difference in keeping you aware of the latest market news and updates. The types of cryptocurrency news and updates that one needs to keep their eyes on include market trends and analysis, regulatory developments and legal updates, new cryptocurrency launches and ICOs, security developments, hacking incidents, and major partnerships and collaborations.

Remember that the market is also highly susceptible to incorrect information and false updates. Therefore, trusting the right information sources is crucial. Instead of relying on unverified sources, you must put your faith in renowned experts and analysts who understand the market better and can also draw correct forecasts and predictions based on historical data and trends. In the highly dynamic cryptocurrency market, getting your hands on the latest updates as soon as possible can make a huge difference to your overall investment returns. When taking your hands on cryptocurrency, the most important element is having a mindset that looks at innovation, embraces disruptive transformation, and can adapt to changing scenarios.

One thing that often gets overlooked is the difference between crypto and Bitcoin investors. Although Bitcoin itself is a cryptocurrency, there is often a variation in the investment behavior and mindset of crypto and bitcoin investors. Since psychology and emotional decision-making tend to play a significant role in the buying and selling of cryptocurrencies, one must understand these factors before entering this space. The two major mindsets dominating the crypto investment market are the "bitcoin or bitcoinist mindset" and the "crypto native mindset."

This mindset is usually common among early Bitcoin adopters who deeply understand the technology and the underlying factors controlling the dynamics in this market. Investors with a bitcoinist mindset believe in the idea of creating a transparent, secure, and decentralized financial system. Their passion for the technology and commitment to Bitcoin projects are visible through their opinions and open support. These are the investors whose primary aim is not to accumulate quick wealth. Rather, their investment decisions are influenced by their strong beliefs in the ideology behind this technology and the future promised by blockchain technology.

On the other hand, crypto natives are investors who have been active crypto users and investors since the inception of cryptocurrencies. They are often active community members and possess a deeper understanding of the market and the factors affecting market movement. These investors openly look for opportunities in the crypto world and are ready to explore the potential applications of blockchain technology and other digital assets. Due to their eagerness to explore the potential of cryptocurrencies, these investors are likely to take financial risks and may be involved in high-risk, high-return investments. Their portfolios consist of multiple currencies and digital assets.

Both investment approaches have their unique pros and cons. Bitcoinists focus only on the use and potential of Bitcoin and may fail to explore the wide range of potential cryptocurrency applications that crypto natives focus on. This is a more cautious and risk-aversive approach, whereas the crypto-native mindset emphasizes an experimental approach for portfolio diversification and profit maximization. However, if not managed efficiently, a crypto-native mindset may lead investors to take uncalculated risks out of fear of missing out (FOMO). The best approach is to adopt a balanced mindset by bridging the gap between these two schools of thought and securing your crypto investments. To make the most of the potential of blockchain and Distributed Ledger Technology (DLT), one needs to develop a growth mindset towards understanding and adopting these technical innovations. This requires exploring the possibilities in this market and the implications or use cases of these technologies for different stakeholders.

This can be sourced from different case studies, reports, news, discussion platforms, research reports, and articles. Developing a growth mindset will help you think critically about the opportunities and risks in the market to make the most of blockchain and DLTs.

An important consideration when exploring the possibilities of cryptocurrencies and blockchain technology is the introduction of web3. *"Web3 is an emergent stack of digital infrastructure powered by technologies such as blockchain, smart contracts, and zero-knowledge proofs."*[141]

The term refers to the next iteration of the internet, built on blockchain technology and controlled by its users. The idea is to build a decentralized internet network built on DLT and blockchain technology, allowing users to control it communally. The technology is anticipated to bring in a new era of the internet, with community-run networks controlling its use and access compared to the existing centralized control by a few corporations. The top three technologies supporting the development and execution of this new internet include blockchain, smart contracts, and digital assets and tokens.

Therefore, it is crucial to understand the nuances of these technologies beforehand to be prepared for the upcoming change.

An important question that arises regarding the nature and potential of cryptocurrency and blockchain is whether they are disruptive or sustaining innovations in the financial sector. Experts have varying views about this. According to a survey conducted among experts, the majority of the respondents believe blockchain to be a sustaining innovation rather than a disruptive innovation.[142] Despite the growing popularity of blockchain technology in the financial world, it is yet to be seen whether it will turn out to be a disruptive or sustaining innovation; however, there is no doubt about its massive growth potential and gains. Bitcoin and Crypto could make you a millionaire with the right mindset and balance of careful research, diversification, time, and some luck.

"Thousands of experts study overbought indicators, head-and-shoulder patterns, put-call ratios, the Fed's policy on money supply…and they can't predict markets with any useful consistency, any more than the gizzard squeezers could tell the Roman emperors when the Huns would attack."

Peter Lynch

Glossary

51% Attack: It is an attack on a blockchain by a group of miners controlling over 50% of a network's mining hash rate.

Algorithm: A process or set of rules to be followed in problem-solving or calculation operations, usually by a computer.

All-time-high (ATH): The highest point in terms of price and market capitalization that a cryptocurrency has been in history.

All-time-low (ATL): The lowest point in terms of price and market capitalization that a cryptocurrency has been in history.

Altcoins: An alternative cryptocurrency other than Bitcoin.

Anti-Money Laundering (AML): A set of international laws to curtail individuals and criminal organizations involved in money laundering through cryptocurrency.

Automated Market Maker (AMM): A decentralized exchange (DEX) protocol that allows users to trade digital assets automatically and without permission. AMMs use liquidity pools instead of a traditional market of buyers and sellers and are part of the decentralized finance (DeFi) ecosystem.

Bitcoin: The first decentralized cryptocurrency.

Bitcoin Core: A free, open-source software that defines the Bitcoin protocol and acts as a standard for the Bitcoin network. It's the original and most widely used Bitcoin client, allowing users to connect to the network, run nodes, and validate blocks and transactions.

Bitcoin halving: An event in which the total rewards per confirmed block halves.

Bitcoin mining: The process by which transactions are officially entered into the blockchain using SHA 256 miners. It is also the way new bitcoins are launched into circulation.

Blockchain: A shared, immutable public ledger that facilitates the process of recording transactions and tracking assets in a business network.

Block reward: The coins awarded to a miner or group of miners for solving the cryptographic problem required to create a new block on a given blockchain.

Burn address: Also known as burning tokens, this is irreversible and typically achieved by sending the coins to a public wallet address where they cannot be retrieved or spent. Once coins are sent to this "burn address," they are effectively rendered unusable, thus reducing the total cryptocurrency circulation supply. Similarly, like a stock buyback.

Central Bank: A public institution that is responsible for implementing monetary policy, managing the currency of a country or group of countries, and controlling the money supply.

Central Bank Digital Currency (CBDC): A CBDC is a digital form of central bank money that is widely available to the general public."Central bank money" refers to money that is a liability of the central bank. In the United States, there are currently two types of central bank money: physical currency issued by the Federal Reserve and digital balances held by commercial banks at the Federal Reserve.

Cold wallet: An entirely offline cryptocurrency wallet.

Consensus algorithm: A process used to achieve agreement on a single data value among distributed processes or systems.

Crypto mixer: A mixer is a conceptual attempt that allows anyone to anonymize their cryptocurrencies by allowing a third party to mix up their crypto with a bunch of other crypto transactions. At the end of the process, after a small fee, it is very difficult to decipher whose crypto and originating wallet address went in and who came out, effectively obscuring the origin of transactions on the blockchain ledger.

Crypto wallet: Digital wallets that store users' public and private keys for their cryptocurrencies.

Custodial wallet: Wallet services offered by a centralized business such as a cryptocurrency exchange.

Dark web: A portion of the internet exists on darknets that are not indexed by search engines and can only be accessed with specific software, configurations, or authorizations such as TOR Projects Onion Browser.

Data validation: Data validation is the process of clarifying the accuracy and quality of a set of data before it is used.

Dead coin: A cryptocurrency integrity that is no longer in existence.

Dead wallet: Dead crypto wallets are cryptocurrency addresses that have been inactive for multiple years.

Debased: A debasement of coinage is the practice of lowering the intrinsic value of coins, primarily when used in connection with commodity money, such as gold or silver coins while continuing to circulate it at face value.

Decentralized: Decentralization refers to the property of a system in which nodes or actors work in concert in a distributed fashion to achieve a common goal.

Decentralized Autonomous Organization (DAO): A group of people who work together toward a shared goal and abide by rules written into the project's self-executing computer code.

Decentralized Exchange (DEX): A peer-to-peer (P2P) marketplace that allows users to trade cryptocurrencies directly with each other without the need for an intermediary. DEXs are a key part of the decentralized finance (DeFi) movement and are non-custodial, meaning users retain control of their private keys. DEXs use smart contracts on a blockchain to automate the trading process.

Decentralized Finance (DeFi): A financial system relying on cryptocurrency and blockchain technology to manage financial transactions.

Dumping: A collective market sell-off that occurs when large quantities of a particular cryptocurrency are sold in a short period.

Elliptic curve cryptography: The secp256k1 method is used to generate public and private key pairs using the formula $y2 = x3 + 7$.

Elliptical Curve Digital Signature Algorithm (ECDSA): A private key is used to produce a public key, but the public key cannot be reverse-engineered to create the private key.

Encryption: The process of converting data into secret, incomprehensible code such that only intended parties are capable of understanding the information. Encryption transforms the original data, known as plaintext, into a secret code known as ciphertext.

Ether: The form of payment used in the operation of the distribution application platform, Ethereum.

Exchange Traded Funds (ETFs): A security that tracks a basket of assets such as stocks, bonds, and cryptocurrencies but can be traded like a single stock.

Fear of Missing Out (FOMO): the anxiety or apprehension that individuals feel when they perceive that others are making profitable investments or taking advantage of significant opportunities in the Cryptocurrency market, and they might miss out on potential gains.

Federal Reserve (FED): The central bank of the United States provides the nation with a safe, flexible, and stable monetary and financial system.

Fiat currency: derived from the Latin word fiat, which means a determination by an authority. In this case, a government decrees the value of the currency, even though it isn't representative of another asset or financial instrument such as gold or a check.

Fork: A fork happens whenever a community makes a change to the blockchain's protocol or fundamental set of rules. When this happens, the chain splits — producing a second blockchain that shares all of its history with the original but is headed off in a new direction.

Fractional reserve banking: A system in which only a fraction of bank deposits are required to be available for withdrawal. Banks only need to keep a specific amount of cash on hand and can create loans from the money you deposit. If you deposit $2,000, your bank might lend 90% of it to other customers with interest, along with 90% from five different customer accounts, creating enough capital to finance $9,000 in loans.

GameFi: The intersection of blockchain technology, decentralized finance (DeFi), and game theory, which combines elements of gaming with financial services.

Hash: A cryptographic function that creates a fixed-length value from a block of data in a blockchain. This value is called a "hash" or "digest" and is unique to the input data. The hash is then added to the end of the chain, creating a digital fingerprint for the block of data.

Hashing algorithm: A mathematical function that mangles data and makes it unreadable.

Hashing function: Used to ensure the blockchain's security and immutability. Each block in the blockchain contains a cryptographic hash of the previous block's data, so modifying data in an earlier block invalidates all subsequent blocks.

Hashpower: (Sometimes called hash rate) A measure of the computational power of a blockchain network, group, or individual. The hash rate is determined by how many guesses are made per second to solve for the hash on a cryptographic blockchain. The overall hash rate helps determine the mining difficulty of a blockchain network.

Hardware wallet: A "cold" cryptocurrency hardware wallet is a physical piece of hardware that exists offline, which allows the user to take control of their cryptographic keys.

Hold On for Dear Life (HODL): An investment strategy of buying cryptocurrency with the intent of never selling it.

Hot wallet: An online wallet that is always connected to the internet.

Inflation: When the money supply in an economy grows at a faster rate than the economy's ability to produce goods and services.

Initial Coin Offering (ICO): A type of crowdfunding using cryptocurrencies as a means of raising capital for early-stage companies.

Intrinsic value: The perceived or calculated value of an asset, investment, or company used in fundamental analysis.

Internet Protocol (IP) address: A unique numeric address assigned to a device connected to the internet.

Know Your Customer (KYC): Security checks completed by trading platforms and crypto exchanges to verify the identity of their customers.

Ledger: A record of transactions maintained by both centralized financial institutions and decentralized finance applications.

Ledger (hardware wallet): Stores your private keys in a secure, offline environment, giving you peace of mind and complete control over your assets. Your private keys are isolated from an internet connection, keeping your wallet protected from hackers and spyware on your laptop or smartphone.

Litecoin: An open-source, global payment network that is fully decentralized without any central authorities.

Memecoin: Crypto tokens created as a joke or meme.

Merged mining: The act of mining two or more cryptocurrencies at the same time without sacrificing overall mining performance.

Merkle Tree: A tree-like data structure that uses cryptographic hashes to encode and verify data.

Mining difficulty adjustment (Bitcoin): A mining difficulty adjustment is a crucial part of the Bitcoin mining process that adjusts the difficulty of the mathematical equation miners must solve to find the next block's hash. The difficulty adjustment happens automatically every 2,016 blocks, or about two weeks, and depends on the number of participants in the mining network and their combined hash power.

Monetary supply: The entire stock of a nation's currency and other liquid instruments in circulation at a given time.

Mt. Gox: A cryptocurrency exchange for buying and selling Bitcoin that was once the world's largest platform for cryptocurrency. The name is an acronym for "Magic: The Gathering Online Exchange," and the site was created in 2010 by Jed McCaleb as a way for fans of the card game to trade cards online. At its peak, Mt. Gox handled 70–80% of Bitcoin trading volume, which gave it a significant role in determining the cryptocurrency's market activity. It is now bankrupt.

Multisig wallet: A multisig wallet, or multi-signature wallet, is a digital wallet that requires multiple users to authorize a transaction. The number of signatures needed to sign a transaction is equal to or less than the number of users, or copayers, who share the wallet. For example, a 2-3 wallet requires two signatures from three copayers, while a 3-3 wallet requires three signatures from three copayers.

Node (blockchain): A device, usually a computer that participates in a blockchain network by running the blockchain protocol's software, allowing it to help validate transactions and keep the network secure.

Non-Fungible Tokens (NFTs): Blockchain-verified assets that cannot be replicated or corrupted.

Private key: A variable in cryptography that is used with an algorithm to encrypt and decrypt data.

Proof-of-stake: A cryptocurrency consensus mechanism for processing transactions and creating new blocks in a blockchain. (Ethereum)

Proof-of-work: A blockchain consensus mechanism that requires significant computing effort from a network of devices. (Bitcoin)

Protocol: The set of rules that define interactions on a network, usually involving consensus, transaction validation, and network participation on a blockchain.

Public key-based digital signatures: Allow users to send Bitcoin trustless.

Pump and dump: A form of fraud involving the artificial inflation of the price of a cryptocurrency with false and misleading positive statements.

Quantitative Easing (QE): a monetary policy strategy used by central banks like the Federal Reserve. With QE, a central bank purchases securities in an attempt to reduce interest rates, increase the supply of money, and drive more lending to consumers and businesses.

Seed key: A sequence of 12 or 24 random words that provide the information required to recover a lost or damaged cryptocurrency wallet.

Self-custodial wallet: A wallet that lets you send and receive crypto and connect to decentralized apps (DApps). With a self-custody wallet, you manage your private key, meaning you have complete control of your crypto assets.

Silk Road: A digital black market platform that was popular for hosting money laundering activities and illegal drug transactions using Bitcoin. Silk Road, regarded as the first darknet market, was launched in 2011 and eventually shut down by the FBI in 2013.

Smart contracts: Digital contracts stored on a blockchain that are automatically executed when predetermined terms and conditions are met.

Software wallet: Also known as a wallet app, is a program that allows users to store, send, and receive cryptocurrencies in a virtual space. Software wallets are encrypted and require a password to access. They can be installed on any device, including phones, tablets, and computers.

Stablecoin: A cryptocurrency whose value is pegged to a real-world fiat asset.

Staking: Crypto staking is a process where investors lock up their crypto tokens with a blockchain validator for a set period to help support the blockchain's operation. In return, investors are rewarded with new tokens when their staked tokens are used to validate blockchain data.

The Onion Router (Tor): a free, open-source browser that uses the Tor network to protect a user's privacy and anonymity while browsing the internet. Its onion routing method involves routing internet traffic through multiple layers of servers to secure data. This process prevents observers from discovering a user's IP address and exact location, and websites and services will only see a connection from the Tor network instead of the user's real IP address.

Tokens: Any cryptocurrency besides Bitcoin and Ethereum representing digital assets residing on their own blockchains.

Token swap: In decentralized finance (DeFi), swapping is the process of exchanging one cryptocurrency for another using a smart contract-based exchange protocol.

Utility token: Blockchain-based tokens that have a specific use and offer utility.

Web 3.0: The third generation of the World Wide Web (WWW), which involves direct immersion into the digital world.

References

[1] Antonopoulos, A. (2017). Mastering Bitcoin: Programming the Open Blockchain. Chapter 2.
https://github.com/bitcoinbook/bitcoinbook/blob/develop/ch02.asciidoc

[2] Antonopoulos, A. (2017). Mastering Bitcoin: Programming the Open Blockchain. Chapter 1.
https://github.com/bitcoinbook/bitcoinbook/blob/develop/ch01.asciidoc

[3] Antonopoulos, A. (2017). Mastering Bitcoin: Programming the Open Blockchain. Chapter 1.
https://github.com/bitcoinbook/bitcoinbook/blob/develop/ch01.asciidoc

[4] Antonopoulos, A. (2017). Mastering Bitcoin: Programming the Open Blockchain. Chapter 2.
https://github.com/bitcoinbook/bitcoinbook/blob/develop/ch02.asciidoc

[5] Antonopoulos, A. (2017). Mastering Bitcoin: Programming the Open Blockchain. Chapter 1.
https://github.com/bitcoinbook/bitcoinbook/blob/develop/ch01.asciidoc

[6] ussc.gov/sites/default/files/pdf/training/annual-national-training-seminar/2018/Emerging_Tech_Bitcoin_Crypto.pdf

[7] ussc.gov/sites/default/files/pdf/training/annual-national-training-seminar/2018/Emerging_Tech_Bitcoin_Crypto.pdf

[8] ussc.gov/sites/default/files/pdf/training/annual-national-training-seminar/2018/Emerging_Tech_Bitcoin_Crypto.pdf

[9] Antonopoulos, A. (2017). Mastering Bitcoin: Programming the Open Blockchain. Chapter 1.
https://github.com/bitcoinbook/bitcoinbook/blob/develop/ch01.asciidoc

[10] ussc.gov/sites/default/files/pdf/training/annual-national-training-seminar/2018/Emerging_Tech_Bitcoin_Crypto.pdf

[11] Antonopoulos, A. (2017). Mastering Bitcoin: Programming the Open Blockchain. Chapter 2.
https://github.com/bitcoinbook/bitcoinbook/blob/develop/ch02.asciidoc

[12] Antonopoulos, A. (2017). Mastering Bitcoin: Programming the Open Blockchain. Chapter 2.
https://github.com/bitcoinbook/bitcoinbook/blob/develop/ch02.asciidoc

[13] Antonopoulos, A. (2017). Mastering Bitcoin: Programming the Open Blockchain. Chapter 1.
https://github.com/bitcoinbook/bitcoinbook/blob/develop/ch01.asciidoc

[14] Antonopoulos, A. (2017). Mastering Bitcoin: Programming the Open Blockchain. Chapter 1. https://github.com/bitcoinbook/bitcoinbook/blob/develop/ch01.asciidoc

[15] Quantitative Easing: An Underappreciated Success | PIIE

[16] Back to Basics: What Is Money? - Finance & Development, September 2012 (imf.org)

[17] Chronology of Monetary History 9,000 - 1 BC (exeter.ac.uk)

[18] What is bitcoin halving? What it means and how it works (usatoday.com)

[19] Off-Ramp and On-Ramp Crypto, What You Need To Know (rockwallet.com)

[20] The Genesis Block: The First Bitcoin Block | Nasdaq

[21] Stevenson University

[22] bitcoinbook/ch01_intro.adoc at develop · bitcoinbook/bitcoinbook · GitHub

[23] bitcoinbook/ch02_overview.adoc at develop · bitcoinbook/bitcoinbook · GitHub

[24] Bitcoin Forum - Index (bitcointalk.org)

[25] Pizza for bitcoins? (bitcointalk.org)

[26] The History of the Mt Gox Hack: Bitcoin's Biggest Heist (blockonomi.com)

[27] What's the dark web? - Google One Help

[28] bitcoin.pdf

[29] 'Bitcoin is a currency': Federal judge says the virtual cash is real money (nbcnews.com)

[30] A Vancouver Coffee Shop Has the World's First Bitcoin ATM (businessinsider.com)

[31] What Are Altcoins, Coins, and Tokens? | Britannica Money

[32] [ANN] Litecoin - a lite version of Bitcoin. Launched! (bitcointalk.org)

[33] Litecoin - Open source P2P digital currency

[34] Orphan block - Glossary | CSRC (nist.gov)

[35] Just a moment... (bitcointalk.org)

[36] Ethereum Launches | Ethereum Foundation Blog

[37] Utility Token Definition | CoinMarketCap

[38] What are Stablecoins and How They Work | Britannica Money

[39] What is the difference between Utility Tokens and Security Tokens? — Bitpanda Academy

[40] Dogecoin - An open-source peer-to-peer digital currency

[41] MasterCoin: New Protocol Layer Starting From "The Exodus Address" (bitcointalk.org)

[42] MasterCoin: New Protocol Layer Starting From "The Exodus Address" (bitcointalk.org)

[43] Cryptocurrency Pump-and-Dump Schemes by Tao Li, Donghwa Shin, Baolian Wang :: SSRN

[44] finma.ch/en/news/2018/02/20180216-mm-ico-wegleitung/

[45] Cryptocurrency Pump-and-Dump Schemes by Tao Li, Donghwa Shin, Baolian Wang :: SSRN

[46] Let's talk about the projected coin supply over the coming years.. : r/ethereum (reddit.com)

[47] $257 Million: Filecoin Breaks All-Time Record for ICO Funding - CoinDesk

[48] wsj.com

[49] What Is a Crypto Winter? | The Motley Fool

[50] Comparative study on cryptocurrency transaction and banking transaction - ScienceDirect

[51] Difference between Traditional V/S Crypto Banking (bitcointalk.org)

[52] What is Tumbler? Definition & Meaning | Crypto Wiki (bitdegree.org)

[53] https://twitter.com/officialmcafee/status/1131907719269634049

[54] bitcoinbook/ch11_blockchain.adoc at develop · bitcoinbook/bitcoinbook · GitHub

[55] " What are smart contracts on blockchain? | IBM

[56] Back to Basics: What Is Money? - Finance & Development, September 2012 (imf.org)

[57] Barter | Barter System, Exchange Economy & Bartering | Britannica Money

[58] https://digitalcommons.bard.edu/cgi/viewcontent.cgi?article=1028&context=senproj_f2022

[59] What Is the Gold Standard? Advantages, Alternatives, and History (investopedia.com)

[60] https://digitalcommons.bard.edu/cgi/viewcontent.cgi?article=1028&context=senproj_f2022#:~:text=This%20paper%20will%20argue%20that,unlike%20the%20Fiat%20Money%20system.

[61] https://www.federalreservehistory.org/essays/panic-of-1907

[62] What Is Quantitative Easing (QE), and How Does It Work? (investopedia.com)

[63] Quantitative easing generates more inflation than conventional monetary policy | CEPR

[64] Bitcoin vs. fiat currencies: Insights from extreme dependence and risk spillover analysis with financial markets - ScienceDirect

[65] What Happens to Bitcoin After All 21 Million Are Mined? (investopedia.com)

[66] (PDF) COMPARATIVE ANALYSIS OF VOLATILITY OF CRYPTOCURRENCIES AND FIAT MONEY (researchgate.net)

[67] PwC Global Crypto Regulation Report 2023 - Amended to include the BCBS rules

[68] What is Anti-Money Laundering? | IBM

[69] Cryptocurrency Income Is Taxable Income - Center for American Progress

[70] Which Countries Have Banned Crypto, and Why? (techopedia.com)

[71] PwC Global Crypto Regulation Report 2023 - Amended to include the BCBS rules

[72] https://www.bis.org/publ/bppdf/bispap136.pdf

[73] Bitcoin's Price History (investopedia.com)

[74] $9 Billion Worth Of Ethereum Was Burned In 1.4 Years | CryptoCrunchApp on Binance Square

[75] Ethereum's Coming of Age: "Dencun" and ETH 2.0 (grayscale.com)

[76] Ethereum's Burn Mechanism: Over $9 Billion in ETH Removed From Supply - UNLOCK Blockchain (unlock-bc.com)

[77] How Much of Your Portfolio Should be in Crypto? (betterment.com)

[78] What Is Dollar Cost Averaging? | Charles Schwab

[79] Deflationary Coins, Tokens, Cryptos & Assets | CryptoSlate

[80] Pepe (PEPE) - Price, Chart, Info | CryptoSlate

[81] Baby Doge Coin (BabyDoge) - Price, Chart, Info | CryptoSlate

[82] Bitcoin's surge to $73k put 99.76% of entities in profit, signaling mature phase of bull market (cryptoslate.com)

[83] Bitcoin price history Mar 24, 2024 | Statista

[84] What is Bitcoin Halving (2024) & How Does it Work? (indiatimes.com)

[85] Tweets from Elon Musk and other celebrities boost dogecoin to record (cnbc.com)

[86] Crypto Market Cap Charts | CoinGecko

[87] https://www.coindesk.com/learn/custodial-wallets-vs-non-custodial-crypto-wallets/

[88] Seed Phrase (crypto.com)

[89] DeFi leverage (bis.org)

[90] Ethereum's Vitalik Buterin Calls on Power Users to Move to Layer 2 Scaling - CoinDesk

[91] What is PancakeSwap (CAKE)? | The Motley Fool

[92] Everything You Need to Know About Binance Smart Chain (BSC) - Blockchain Council (blockchain-council.org)

[93] Polygon blockchain explained: A beginner's guide to MATIC (cointelegraph.com)

[94] Polygon blockchain explained: A beginner's guide to MATIC (cointelegraph.com)

[95] General | Tangible

[96] What is GameFi and How Does Play-to-Earn Work? (techopedia.com)

[97] The Metaverse, Zuckerberg's Tech Obession, Is Officially Dead. ChatGPT Killed It. (businessinsider.com)

[98] Different Ways to Verify Your Smart Contract Code | QuickNode

[99] SEC.gov | Statement on the Approval of Spot Bitcoin Exchange-Traded Products

[100] SEC Pushes Back on ETH ETF Applications From BlackRock, Fidelity (coindesk.com)

[101] Masterworks - Learn to Invest in Fine Art

[102] Cryptocurrency Market Size, Growth & Trends Report, 2030 (fortunebusinessinsights.com)

[103] Day Trading: Leveraging Stop Loss Orders for Intraday Trading Success - FasterCapital

[104] What Does HODL Mean in Crypto? | The Motley Fool

[105] What Is Crypto Mining? Overview, Benefits, & Risks | Britannica Money

[106] Crypto Staking Explained: How It Works, Types, & Risks | Britannica Money

[107] How Does Bitcoin Mining Work? A Guide for Business | Toptal®

[108] bitcoinbook/ch01_intro.adoc at develop · bitcoinbook/bitcoinbook · GitHub

[109] How is SHA-256 used in blockchain, and why? (educative.io)

[110] Bitcoin Mining Evolution: CPUs, ASICs & Merged Mining | Rootstock - Smart Contract Platform Secured by the Bitcoin Network

[111] Hash Functions and list/types of Hash functions - GeeksforGeeks

[112] GPU Mining Definition | Forexpedia™ by BabyPips.com

[113] Merged Mining | Binance Academy

[114] What Is a 51% Attack? (coindesk.com)

[115] Mining — Bitcoin

[116] (PDF) Revisiting Bitcoin's carbon footprint (researchgate.net)

[117] bitcoinbook/ch12_mining.adoc at develop · bitcoinbook/bitcoinbook · GitHub

[118] Bitcoin snuck into the Billions season 5 premiere. Here's how - Decrypt

[119] Crypto Mining Taxes: Beginner's Guide 2024 | CoinLedger

[120] bitcoinbook/ch02_overview.adoc at develop · bitcoinbook/bitcoinbook · GitHub

[121] (PDF) Revisiting Bitcoin's carbon footprint (researchgate.net)

[122] Carbon Footprint Comparison of Bitcoin and Conventional Currencies in a Life Cycle Analysis Perspective - ScienceDirect

[123] How one Pennsylvania company is using waste coal to mine Bitcoin (alleghenyfront.org)

[124] Is Proof-of-Stake Really More Energy-Efficient Than Proof-of-Work? (bitwave.io)

[125] Yield Farming: The Truth About This Crypto Investment Strategy (investopedia.com)

[126] thestreet.com

[127] Bitcoin Halving Countdown Live (watcher.guru)

[128] How Many Bitcoin Are There? How Much Supply Left to Mine? (bitbo.io)

[129]

B11___SC_LY__BOOK_CHAPTER___Environmental_effects_of_Cryptocurrenci es[1].pdf (dcu.ie)

[130] SEC.gov | Statement on the Approval of Spot Bitcoin Exchange-Traded Products

[131] What Is a Central Bank Digital Currency (CBDC)? (investopedia.com)

[132] Blockchain application for central bank digital currencies (CBDC) - PMC (nih.gov)

[133] https://www.gov.cn/zhengce/content/2014-06/27/content_8913.htm

[134] China banned millions of people with poor social credit from transportation in 2018 - The Verge

[135] The complicated truth about China's social credit system | WIRED

[136] Coming soon: America's own social credit system | The Hill

[137] CBDCs Will Be the End of American Freedom | Opinion (newsweek.com)

[138] III. The future monetary system (bis.org)

[139] BlackRock's Game-Changing Bitcoin ETF: What Every Investor Needs to Know | The Motley Fool

[140] https://cryptoadventure.com/will-altcoins-overtake-bitcoin-investment-returns-in-the-future/

[141] https://www.sciencedirect.com/science/article/pii/S219985312300152X

[142] https://sloanreview.mit.edu/strategy-forum/is-blockchain-a-disruptive-or-a-sustaining-innovation-what-experts say/

Made in the USA
Las Vegas, NV
17 December 2024

14646511R00128